Air Rifle Shooting

Air Rifle Shooting

for Pest Control and Rabbiting

JOHN BEZZANT

THE CROWOOD PRESS

First published in 2009 by
The Crowood Press Ltd
Ramsbury, Marlborough
Wiltshire SN8 2HR

www.crowood.com

British Library Cataloguing-in-Publication Data
A catalogue record for this book is available from the British Library.

ISBN 978 1 84797 043 5

Disclaimer
The author and the publisher do not accept any responsibility in any manner whatsoever for any error or omission, nor any loss, damage, injury or liability of any kind incurred as a result of the use of any of the information contained in this book, or reliance upon it.

Acknowledgements
I should like to acknowledge Peter Martineau of BSA Guns and Tony Gibson of Deben Group Industries for their invaluable technical support and advice in the production of the book.

Credits
All photographs by David Bezzant.
Line drawings by Keith Field.

Designed by Bookcraft Limited, Stroud, Gloucestershire

Printed and bound in Malaysia by Times Offset (M) Sdn Bhd.

Contents

CHAPTER ONE

Teaching Yourself to Shoot an Air Rifle

THE AIR RIFLE'S PURPOSE

There are two tasks to which the air rifle is generally put: pest control and rabbit hunting.

Pest Control

Pest control often takes place in barns or industrial buildings. Using a firearm or shotgun in such locations would obviously lead to serious damage occurring to the fabric of the building. This would make you most unpopular with the property's owner, but beyond this there is the question of safety.

Pest control takes place at very close range, so any weapon more powerful than an air rifle will send its projectile zipping straight through the quarry like a missile. It has more than enough surplus energy remaining to cause serious, even fatal, injuries to stock, farm workers, or the shooter himself.

Within buildings, the use of firearms is highly likely to result in ricochets. This occurs when a projectile passes clean though the quarry, strikes something hard (such as a wall) and bounces off it. The shooter has absolutely no control over a ricocheting bullet: it can go anywhere.

In barns and industrial buildings, there may be animals or people in the locality; this, combined with the ricochet factor, is a recipe for disaster. It is also entirely possible that the person firing the gun could end up being the one that gets hurt. I know of an incident in which a highly trained soldier was killed by a ricocheting bullet fired from his own weapon. Only an incompetent fool would choose to use a firearm within the confines of a building.

Another problem with firearms, when it comes to pest control, is the fact that they are not able to deal with the large number of pigeons that have to be taken in one go. In a morning I can take forty pigeons from a single building. In the larger industrial buildings, it is possible to take a hundred or more pigeons in quick succession. The reason for this is that a firearm discharges its projectile by causing a small, controlled explosion within the barrel. A side-effect of the explosion is heat, which will shortly start to have a detrimental effect upon the weapon's accuracy. As few as ten to fifteen rounds can be sufficient to affect accuracy. Air weapons do not have this problem: they can fire a hundred pellets in quick succession without their accuracy being affected.

Rabbit Hunting

Several factors make the air rifle, rather than a firearm, a more suitable weapon for rabbit hunting. Firstly, landowners are often willing to let a person on to their land to hunt rabbits with an air rifle, but would not be willing to grant that same permission to someone with a firearm. They understandably believe that the potential for accidental injury or damage to property is far greater when a firearm is employed.

Secondly, quite a lot of land is not suitable for the use of firearms. This includes fields with roads or footpaths near by, or fields that back on to houses. Any fields that contain stock or surround a farmhouse or farm buildings will probably be off limits. Not so with the air rifle.

A firearm may outstrip an air rifle for sheer power and range, but that power has a downside. Any shot that misses a rabbit can travel a considerably long way, 220yd (200m), say. As a consequence, a firearms user has to satisfy himself that behind every target he shoots at there is something that can act as a backstop to absorb the bullet if it misses the target.

A bullet is a lethal projectile. Therefore, the shooter has to be 100 per cent positive that a miss will find the bullet going to ground long before it reaches an environment where it can do any damage. This places a very high degree of responsibility upon the shooter. Air rifles do not present the shooter with that kind of responsibility, meaning that the shooter can discharge an air rifle with a far greater degree of confidence. This is a point well worth considering: a stray bullet that causes damage or injury will expose the shooter to criminal prosecution and/or possible civil litigation.

Air rifles have to be used with care, but their lower power levels make them a lot safer to use than firearms. A firearm will exhibit a muzzle energy of about 1,000ft per lb. A non-FAC (Firearms Certificated) rated air rifle will, in comparison, produce no more than 12ft per lb muzzle energy. Even an FAC-rated air rifle will not go much above 40–80ft per lb. These figures dramatically demonstrate how much safer an air rifle is to use than a firearm.

Firearms are very noisy. Even your humble .22's noise scares those who are not used to hearing it; it also scares dogs and livestock. But a modern air rifle fitted with a state-of-the-art silencer hardly manages to whisper. This has obvious advantages. Firstly, you will not scare the landowner or his neighbours; secondly, you won't scare off every rabbit for miles around when you discharge the weapon.

COMPARISONS

At the time of writing, a decent .22 bullet rifle will set you back in the region of £500 to £600, whereas an air rifle of similar quality can be purchased for £250 to £350. But the real saving comes with the ammunition. Pellets are a tenth of the price of the cheapest bullets.

A shotgun, unlike an air rifle, can be used to take moving targets. This is because the shotgun spreads its load over a wide area. However there is a downside: the quarry is peppered with hundreds of tiny pieces of shot. The person preparing the meat for the table may be very diligent indeed but, no matter how hard they try to remove all the shot, some of it always remains undetected – most unpleasant to discover in the mouth when you're eating. An air rifle delivers a much more surgical strike, because only a single pellet is used to take down the quarry, usually in the head –a part of the animal that is not eaten.

How Clean is the Kill?

Many people think that the low level of power produced by an air rifle means that these weapons do not have sufficient punch to kill an animal cleanly. A non-FAC-rated air rifle can have a maximum muzzle energy of 12ft per lb; it only takes 4ft per lb to kill a rabbit if shot in the head. So when a pellet leaves the barrel of an air rifle, it has three times more energy than that required to kill a rabbit. But it's not quite as simple as that: a pellet on its flight from barrel to target constantly loses energy as a result of drag.

What we need to know is, how much of that initial 12ft per lb will be left when the pellet eventually strikes the rabbit's head. This depends upon the range and upon the type of pellet you use, but the following table gives a fair indication.

From the chart overleaf you can see that even at 40yd (36m), the air rifle can deliver a pellet with almost twice the level of energy required to kill a rabbit.

The effect of range on energy levels	
Range	*Feet per pound*
20yd (18m)	9½
30yd (27m)	8.6
40yd (36m)	7.7

THE AIR RIFLE HUNTER

Is it possible for a complete beginner to teach himself how to shoot? Yes, but it won't be a walk in the park. This book has been put together in such a way that it can be used as a self-teaching training manual, equipping you with everything you need to know to become a competent hunter.

Hunting quarry with an air rifle has to be humanely carried out. Thus, the air rifle user must be a competent marksman. To become a marksman involves a lot of work, and discipline akin to that exhibited by those who engage in athletic sports. You have to know how ammunition behaves, be thoroughly conversant with the workings of telescopic sights, have the ability to read the weather, possess a broad knowledge of animal behaviour, be able to utilize fieldcraft to blend into the outdoor environment in which you are hunting, and finally be able to handle your chosen weapon.

All the required skills have a theoretical element that must be tackled through the avenue of serious study. Then there is the practical side: hours upon hours of practice are necesssary if you want to turn all the hard-won theory into a usable skill.

Marksmanship is a skill acquired by those who commit a large amount of time to long practice sessions on the range; this hones the skills to the level required by those who want to shoot at living creatures. Marksmanship is a perishable skill, and if you do not practise on a regular basis it will fade. Competitive target shooters will practise every single day to keep their skills in tip-top condition. The serious hunter needs to be finding the time for at least one session on the range every week.

Attributes

In addition to the hours of practice, there are some personal qualities that an individual requires if he is to become a competent hunter. Many people go and spend a small fortune on an air rifle and accessories in order to take up air rifle hunting, only to discover that they are not at all suited to the sport. To save you wasting your money, I have put together a checklist of the physical and emotional qualities that the hunter needs to possess. When looking at this list of attributes, try to be brutally honest with yourself to discover if you are the type of person that can enjoy hunting.

Good Physical Health
Hunting and pest control require the shooter to spend extensive periods of time in the outdoors, often having to combat inclement weather conditions. It is not uncommon to cover anywhere between 5–13km (3–8 miles), on foot, in a morning. Such walking requires a decent degree of physical fitness, specifically strong legs and a good cardio-vascular system. An unfit hunter will succumb to fatigue, which has a detrimental effect upon marksmanship. Good physical condition will mean sharp reflexes and good muscle control, both essential ingredients in the recipe for a good marksman.

Good Vision
Eyesight is obviously one of the marksman's most vital tools. Therefore, good eyesight is essential. This does not preclude those wearing glasses, as long as the glasses are able to give the wearer a normal range of vision.

A Strong Sense of Personal Responsibility
Air weapons are very powerful weapons, so should be handled by those who possess an innate sense of personal responsibility. Those who handle an air rifle must do so in such a way that it does not endanger others or cause any suffering to the quarry. Sadly, vast numbers

of rifles are in the hands of those who do not posses this quality, which is why so many air rifles are used in so many crimes. As a result, it is likely that in the not too distant furture possession of an air rifle will require a licence.

Emotional Toughness
Using air rifles to shoot quarry involves the taking of life, which is not, and should never be, pleasant. There will be blood, and sometimes there will be injured quarry that you will have to finish off with your bare hands.

Being able to deal with this requires a degree of emotional toughness, which does not mean that you must have a cruel streak, but that you must be able to kill in a calm, rational manner. Anxiety and fear of remorse will make you a hesitant shot, resulting in injuries rather than clean kills.

A Feeling for the Outdoors
To become a good sporting marksman able to take quarry cleanly, you will need to acquire a high level of fieldcraft. Aquiring this is possible only if you are a person who enjoys being in the outdoors.

CONSTRUCTING YOUR OWN 40-YARD RANGE

Before you can even contemplate firing an air rifle, you have to provide yourself with a suitable practice area. This means a properly constructed practice range, with sufficient length to allow the shooter to place a target 40yd (36m) away from the firing position. The range does not have to be any longer than 40yd (36m), as this is the absolute maximum range at which quarry should be taken. The rationale behind shooting on a properly constructed range is quite simple.

Modern hunting air rifles are powerful weapons specifically designed to kill. This means that a pellet fired from such a rifle has the capacity to penetrate tissue and smash through thin layers of bone, including those of a human. Usually, when a person is hit accidentally with an air rifle pellet, it is nothing more than a painful flesh wound. But wounds causing permanent disability, even death, are not unknown.

It is clear that practice sessions must take place on a range, and that a bit of board propped up precariously in the back garden is totally inappropriate. You may choose to join a club to access such a range, or you may, like me, decide to build your own. But before going on to the actual construction of the range, it's well worth pausing for a moment to answer a reasonable question that is often posed: Why begin with targets?

Targets
It is essential that you restrict yourself to shooting targets until you are competent enough to hunt live animals. They are the ones that will suffer horribly if you make a hash of it. Very few people are naturally gifted marksmen. For most, marksmanship is a skill hard won through hours of dedicated practice. If you were to go straight out into the field and start shooting at rabbits or birds you would have few, if any, kills. You would also cause an awful lot of suffering to the creatures that you would undoubtedly injure in some way, resulting in a slow, lingering death.

An air rifle pellet is a light, small projectile. It can only cause sufficient shock and injury for instant death if it is accurately placed into a small area of the quarry's body, referred to as the kill zone – usually the head area.

The kill zone will be no bigger than a pound coin. Hitting that at a distance of 30–40yd (25–35m) takes a considerable amount of skill. To acquire this skill, you will have to begin with targets and put in weeks of serious training, sticking at it until you achieve a 1in (25mm) grouping – considered the benchmark for humane hunting. This means being able to place three consecutive shots into an area that can be covered by a 1in (25mm) circle.

Siting Your Range
I live on a smallholding with a five acre field behind the house, so finding somewhere for my range presented me with no problems.

However, if you don't live on a smallholding don't worry; your garden may well suffice if it can spare you an area 40yd (36m) long and 6½ft (2m) wide. In fact, you could just get away with an area slightly smaller: 30yd (27m) long and 1yd (1m) wide.

A garden is private property; if you are the owner of that property you have a legal right to shoot on it as long as your shots do not stray onto other people's land – they won't if you have a properly constructed range.

A modern air rifle fitted with a silencer is very quiet, so neighbours should not be disturbed by your practice sessions as long as you are sensible in your selection of targets. A pellet passes clean through a paper target silently, but a metal target, of which there are many on the market, will produce a plinking sound every time you strike it: a sound that will quickly grow irritating. Think before you shoot.

Range Layout

The piece of ground that you select for your range site needs to measure 30–40yd (25–35m) in length, and 1–2yd (m) in width. It is self-evident that the area chosen has to offer a clear line of sight from the shooting position to the target area. A flat piece of ground could be used, preferably it should have a steady slope from the target area down towards the shooter. Should you miss the backstop, a most unlikely event, the pellet will be caught by the high ground.

The area behind the backstop should be designated a safe zone: 20yd (18m) in depth and 10ft (9m) in width, in which nothing that could be damaged or hurt resides: a greenhouse or grazing cow for example. The safe zone should be open fields or the like. Some modern air rifles can propel a pellet out to a distance of 60yd (55m). In the unlikely event that you miss the backstop, the 20yd (18m) safe zone ensures that the pellet loses all of its remaining energy in an environment that is under your control.

If you do not have sufficient room to facilitate a safe zone behind the range, you can

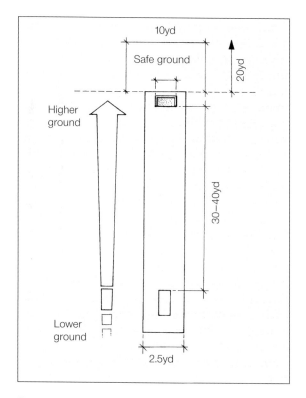

Range layout.

increase the width and height of your backstop: from 4 × 4ft to 6 × 6ft (1.5m × 1.5m to 2m × 2m). Nobody could possibly miss a backstop of that size.

The area between the shooting position and the backstop should be grass or earth, not a hard surface such as concrete. Hard surfaces can cause ricochets which are unpredictable in nature and thus dangerous. The range area should be completely fenced in, so as to prevent pets or people wandering into the line of fire during practice sessions.

Safe handling of an air weapon is the foundation stone on which marksmanship is built. In the RAF, where I learnt to shoot in the 1980s, safety was hammered into me over and over again until it became instinctive; only with this kind of approach can you ensure that accidents do not happen. A bit of wood or a cardboard box propped up in the back garden for practice sessions just will not do.

Constructing the Backstop

A backstop is basically a wall with sides made out of stout material, such as bricks or wood, which is filled with a substance that can absorb a pellet in flight bringing its forward momentum to a rapid halt. Sand is usually that substance, but earth would do just as well as long as it's stone free. One stone in the soil, even a small pebble, could cause a ricochet. The way to ensure that the soil is stone free is to sieve it.

The earth or sand has to have sufficient depth so as to prevent a pellet passing through. The earth or sand is required to be 4in (10cm) at its shallowest point. To achieve this the slope must begin with a base of 2ft (50cm), which will decrease slowly as it grows in height, reducing to 4in (10cm) in depth when it peaks at a height of 3ft (1m). This will require a good tonne of soil or sand.

Constructing the Firing Position

The firing position is simply a place from which you shoot. It should be precisely 30yd (27m) or 40yd (36m) away from the base of the backstop. The firing position can be a small shelter that protects the shooter from the weather, or simply a board on which to kneel or lie. Whichever option you decide to use, it is a good idea to have a couple of firing supports: one to correspond to the kneeling position and another to the standing position.

Wind Indicators and Distance Markers

To finish the range off properly you need to add a couple of wind indicators and a series of range markers. Wind indicators are there to tell you which direction the wind is coming from and how strongly it is blowing, which is vital information that is key to the correct placement of the shot. A wind indicator is easily made by placing a baton to either side of the backstop. The baton should be about 6½ft (2m) in length, with a thin 1ft (30cm) length of lightweight material attatched to the top of it.

Range markers are offcuts of wood painted in a bright colour. They are knocked into the ground along the edge of the range at precise distances (in yards) from the firing position: 10, 15, 20, 25, 30 and 40. The ability to judge

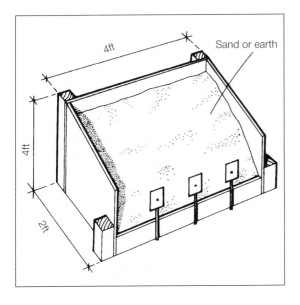

Construction of backstop.

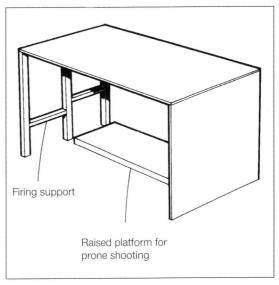

Construction of a firing position.

11

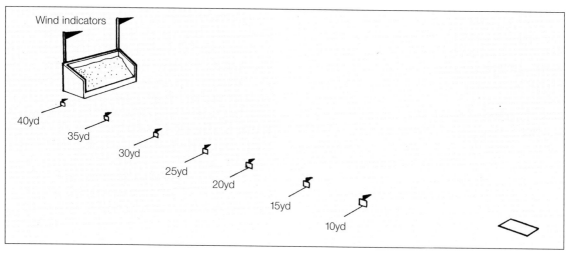

Wind indicators

40yd
35yd
30yd
25yd
20yd
15yd
10yd

Wind indicators and distance markers.

distances to within a few inches is of the utmost importance, as it will enable you to place your shot on the correct trajectory to strike the target at the required mark. The closer something is, the lower you aim; the further away something is, the higher you aim. The distance markers will help to teach you the skill of range-finding.

TARGETS

Now that you have a safe place to shoot you will need something to shoot at. Targets are the obvious choice, but what sort? There are so many to choose from.

To begin with, you will need some traditional-type targets with a number of rings that decrease in size as they move toward the centre. These targets will be needed to set the sights on your rifle, including both open and telescopic sights. These targets will allow you to calculate the adjustments that need to be made to the sight's windage and elevation settings, so that you can calibrate the sights to suit the individualities of your eye. Do not worry – this is not as complicated as it sounds.

When you have learnt the basics, you will need to move on to a target that depicts the type of quarry you intend to shoot. These targets should be life-sized, with the kill

Range Safety

Before you can start to put your newly constructed range to good use, you must first have a clear understanding of range safety. The 'dos and don'ts' that must be followed at all times

- Always have the barrel of the rifle pointing down the range; even when you know for a fact that the weapon is unloaded.
- Always have the safety catch applied until you are in the firing position and ready to take aim.
- Never leave a loaded weapon unattended.
- Always wear safety glasses in case of a ricochet. Ricochets on a properly constructed range are most unlikely, but the unlikely does sometimes happen and if struck in the eye, the shooter may be blinded for life. Safety glasses for shooting purposes can be purchased very cheaply.
- Never allow anyone to enter the range area whilst firing is taking place.

zone of the animal or bird depicted by a small discreet circle. I do not like targets that have the kill zone depicted in some vivid colour that can be seen from miles away. Real quarry does not come with a red dot stuck to its vulnerable areas, so they must reflect reality. Realistic

Target placement.

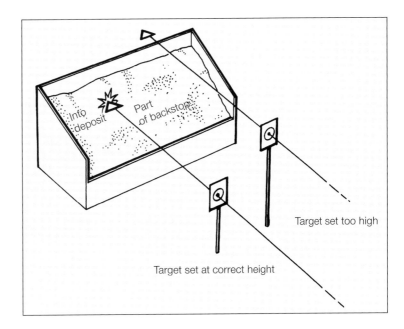

targets will not only reveal the level of your marksmanship, but will give you a good idea of what the real thing will look like at different distances. This is why you will need to practise on the target across the full spectrum, from 10yd (9m) right out to 40yd (36m).

The final type of target that's worth having for the range are the knock-down metal targets used by field target shooters. These targets are the silhouette of an animal or bird cut in metal; somewhere on the silhouette a 1in (25mm) hole is drilled out; behind it a disk is inserted that is connected to a knock-down mechanism. Hit the disk and the target falls down flat, it can be reset by pulling on a length of cord. These targets are great fun for practice sessions.

With paper or card targets you will need something to hold them; all four corners have to be held down or they will blow up in the wind. You could pin your paper target to a board with drawing pins, but it seems a waste of a good wood, especially when a simple target holder can be purchased quite cheaply. The target holder is made of metal rods which, when screwed together, form a cross shape with two crossbars; the bottom is adjustable so that the holder can accept any size of

target. Use bulldog clips to fasten the target between the two crossbars. The target holder has a three-pronged foot on the bottom of its upright, which enables it to be driven easily into the ground. A target holder like this can be acquired from Deben Group Industries (*see* page 148).

Target placement upon the range must be carried out with great care. Whether the target is right at the base of the backstop or just 10yd (9m) away from the shooting position, you want to make sure that the centre part of the target lines up with the deepest part of the backstop. This will give plenty of leeway should you happen to fire a bit too high. If you set your target too high, then a high shot will go straight over the range.

CHOOSING A RIFLE

Now that you have constructed your range and set up a few targets, you need to choose a weapon that you can learn to shoot with. Basically speaking there are two main types of air rifle: those powered by a spring piston and those powered by a compressed air cylinder. The latter are known as pre-charged pneumatics (or PCP for short).

Spring-Piston Rifles (Springers)

When you pull the trigger on a spring-powered rifle, the depressed trigger operates a lever that releases the spring piston; this hurtles down its chamber forcing air into the barrel, thus sending the pellet on its merry way. The release of the spring causes a dynamic reaction known as recoil, which simply means that the rifle moves when fired.

There are three distinct phases to this movement. Firstly, the rifle moves backwards into the shoulder in reaction to the air being forced from the cylinder. Secondly, the backwards movement is then almost instantaneously met and overcome by the forward momentum, created by the spring travelling

violently forward. Thirdly, when the spring hits the front of the cylinder like an express train, it rebounds and the force is once more in a backwards direction.

This movement of the gun (recoil), has to be skilfully managed by the shooter or it will have a devastating effect on accuracy. In short, the recoil of a spring-powered rifle forces the shooter to adopt proper techniques, as it is a most unforgiving weapon that will not tolerate the slightest error in technique.

The PCP Rifle

The PCP has no recoil and is therefore very easy to shoot, being incredibly forgiving of poor technique. With a PCP it is possible to achieve a passable level of accuracy whilst exhibiting a fairly poor technique, though to become a really good shot the technique has to be brought up to scratch. Learning to shoot with a PCP is a bit like learning to drive in an automatic car because the gun does a lot of the work for you.

So which should you choose: a spring-powered or a PCP? Many experts tell you that there is no difference in accuracy between them, which is true enough if you happen to be an expert marksman. (There are guys out there who can split the atom with a single shot.) For the complete beginner and the mere mortal, that is not the case at all.

I have recently been coaching a young lad who had never used an air rifle in his life before. I started him out with a PCP, and after only two half-hour lessons he was beginning to pull together a reasonable grouping. When, however, we moved on to a spring-powered weapon the target looked like it had been peppered by a shotgun. Spring-powered weapons with their violent recoil are much harder to tame than any PCP.

I find that a PCP can give me a tighter grouping than I can achieve with a spring-gun. With the very best PCPs, I am able to put a succession of three shots almost through the same hole on the target. So yes, it is true that tremendous accuracy can be achieved with the spring-powered weapon in the hands

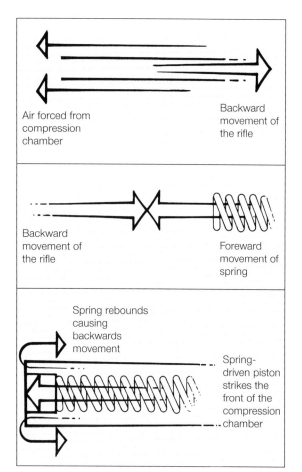

Recoil phase.

of a really good technician. But that kind of skill does not come easily – to some it never comes at all – the only way to purchase such skill is to spend hours upon hours practising on the range.

The late John Darling, an airgun hunter of great renown, used a very powerful spring-powered weapon for many years with great success. However, when the first really good PCP came along the springer was shelved and the PCP took its place.

PCP or Springer?

I am quite a fan of spring-powered weapons. One of my biggest pigeon bags ever was taken with a very simple medium-powered springer, but it has to be said that PCPs are an awful lot easier to use. I just cannot achieve the levels of accuracy with a springer that I can with a PCP. Some may say that the reason for this is that my technique is not good enough, but you just have to take a look at the scores at any field target shoot, and you will see that those using PCPs are achieving higher scores than those using springers.

One of the other problems you will face with a springer derived from its violent recoil: a more frequent loss of zero than occurs with a PCP. Basically, the springer's recoil shakes the rifle aboutabout, which moves the cross-hairs fractionally away from the line to which you zeroed them. They will have to be reset. The PCP does not have such bad behaviour.

Before you go off with the idea that spring-powered weapons are a total waste of time, being more trouble than they are worth, let me highlight their good points. Price for example, a good spring-powered rifle can cost half the price of a PCP, which is an important consideration as not everybody can afford the £400 to £700 price tag that most PCPs carry (in 2008).

Not only is the springer cheap in comparison to a PCP, it is a much simpler form of construction, therefore it takes less skill to maintain and repair; putting it within the scope of the moderately competent DIY-type, operating out of a garden shed or garage. Moreover,

if rifle customizing is your particular interest then the springer is the chap for you, as there is so much that you can do to it.

A springer is also, owing to its simplicity, more rugged than the PCP and will cope better with rough handling.

My rifles take a real hammering in the field, I give them no quarter whatsoever. They are exposed to all kinds of weather, they get filthy, knocked against hard objects and rested on all kinds of surfaces that are abrasive to wood and metal. In my experience, the springer endures such treatment more manfully than the PCP. Knowing that my kind of shooting – crawling around farmyards and clambering over rubbish tips – is so brutal on a gun I prefer to spend less on a weapon, which rules out most PCPs. I can get a good springer that will last for years more cheaply than I can buy a PCP.

Another advantage that the springer has over the PCP, is its independence. The springer is totally self-powered, all it requires is a few good arm muscles to force back the spring, the PCP needs an air source. That air can be provided by an air-cylinder or a hand-operated stirrup pump. The PCP is therefore not a pick up and go weapon, it needs to be charged prior to use. Whereas, the springer is constantly ready for action, nothing needs to be done: just take it and go. This is one of the reasons why so many busy pest control operatives opt for a springer. To help you decide which is the best rifle for you, consider the following points.

Budget
Know exactly how much money you have in the kitty to spend on a rifle. Do not get trapped in the idea that the more expensive the rifle the bigger the bags will be; that is not the case at all. Some of my biggest bags have been had with a secondhand BSA Meteor, bought for less than £80; some of my smallest bags have been taken with a top of the range PCP retailing for a staggering £740. So just forget the notion that money equals success: the more expensive guns may be easier to use but they are not going to increase the bags.

Another thing to bear in mind is that the appearance of a rifle is irrelevant. Airgun manufacturers put a lot of effort into turning out aesthetic works of art to attract the eye. Looks are, from a hunting or pest control perspective, of no importance. Performance is all that matters when you are in the field; a beautiful walnut stock and gleaming metalwork do not kill rabbits. An accurate barrel, crisp action and heavy knock-down power are the things that count. Ask yourself what it can do, not how attractive it is. Multi-shot weapons are obviously more expensive than the single-shot ones, so does the hunter or the pest controller have to have a weapon with a multi-shot capacity to achieve results?

Having a multi-shot capacity does obviously make things somewhat easier. There is no fumbling around for the next pellet – it's there in the magazine waiting to be deployed – which is supremely helpful if you happen to injure your quarry because you can quickly take a second shot. But you do not need a multi-shot weapon to achieve satisfactory results.

I remember last year taking my single-shot BSA Meteor to a cattleshed full of feral pigeons. I took forty-five of them in just a few hours, so you don't have to have a repeating rifle to fill your bag.

A repeating rifle is a pure luxury item, something that is nice to own and use, but no more successful at killing quarry than a more wholesome single-shot weapon.

Before making a final decision, ask yourself what kind of shooting you are going to be involved in – the kind of environment rather than the quarry you are seeking. Is the environment going to be reasonably clean and kind to your weapon, or is it going to be dirty and brutal? If your shooting falls into the latter category, do you really want to be spending the price of a reasonable secondhand car on a PCP?

Pretty woodwork and shiny metal do not stay that way for long once employed in a rugged environment, at least they don't with me up here on the northeast coast of Scotland. Which is why all that I am interested in is practicality not looks. Looks fade rapidly; practicality endures.

SHOOTING TECHNIQUE

The Hold

I shall look at the hold in four basic firing positions, which are the prone position, the kneeling position, the standing position and the sitting position. Learning these four positions should give you sufficient scope to meet most of the situations you encounter whilst hunting or carrying out pest-control operations.

The sniper training manual used by the American forces states that the sniper should always provide the rifle with an artificial support. This means that the sniper should not try to support the rifle by the efforts of

The unassisted prone position: there is nothing but human endeavour to support the rifle.

The unassisted kneeling position.

Like the sniper, the hunter and pest controller should, where possible, use an assisted hold to make his shot, as it is simply the most accurate way to shoot. But there is a problem with spring-powered weapons because they do not like being rested on a firm surface. Hard surfaces resist the rifle's natural recoil cycle, causing the pellet to veer dramatically away from the point of aim. There are, however, a few things that can be done about this.

There are bipods designed to be used with spring-powered weapons. A bipod is basically two legs that are attached to the barrel; it has dampers that prevent it from resisting the rifle's recoil. These days, all sniper weapons are fitted with a bipod because they provide such a stable platform from which to take the shot: every airgunner should make a bipod a part of his basic kit.

When using a spring-powered rifle, I carry in my pocket a sand sock – an old sock filled with builders' sand and tied around the top with a piece of cord to prevent the sand escaping. (The finished article resembles a cosh, so

his body alone, but he should find something to rest the rifle upon. This is known as an assisted hold, which can be employed in the prone, kneeling or standing position.

The reason for employing an assisted hold is to counter the effects of something called 'wobble'. When holding a rifle unassisted, no matter how good the technique, the effort of holding the rifle in the firing position places the muscles under a degree of tension, causing the arms to shake very slightly. This wobble obviously has a detrimental effect upon accuracy. If wobble is not controlled you will never hit the centre of a target. Good technique can heavily reduce the effects of wobble, but resting the rifle on a solid object can almost eradicate the influence that wobble has on a shot.

The unassisted standing position.

An alternative sitting position for the less flexible like me.

make sure you don't wander around in public places with it still in your pocket or you might end up having to do some explaining to the police.) The sand sock can be placed on top of any suitable hard surface that provides a rest for the rifle – the top of a fence post or a car bonnet – the rifle's barrel is then placed upon the sock and the sand prevents the rifle from being affected by the hard surface beneath.

If you are using a PCP a sand sock is not necessary, PCPs can rest happily on any kind of surface, hard or soft, without being affected in the least.

Very occasionally there isn't anything around to act as a support. On such occasions it may be necessary to use an unassisted hold; these take a lot more skill to master than an unassisted hold and should only be used as a last resort. The percentage of first-shot strikes, when comparing assisted and unassisted holds, is dramatically higher for the assisted hold.

One of the main objectives of the airgun shooter is to take his quarry cleanly with the first shot; the assisted hold is the best way to achieve this objective.

Shoulder

Taking up a good firing position is all about bringing the body and the rifle together in a way that does not place undue stress on the muscles. The greater the degree of stress the greater the degree of wobble.

The first thing to realize about the body is that a natural pocket exists between the deltoid muscle and the neck rotators. This pocket is where you place the butt of your rifle. The second thing, is that the butt is designed to configure with the shoulder (the more up-market the stock the greater the degree of configuration it offers). Some guns even have an adjustable butt-plate so that it can be made to marry up to the specific peculiarities of your shoulder pocket. If you can afford a gun with this feature it is well worth considering, as the better the fit between the rifle and body, the greater the level of accuracy you are able to achieve.

You can have a pad sewn into your shooting jacket where the butt goes. It does not reduce the effects of recoil but minimizes the effect of

An unassisted kneeling position.

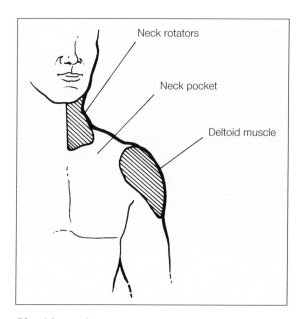

Shoulder pocket.

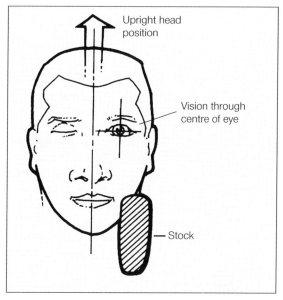

Correct head position.

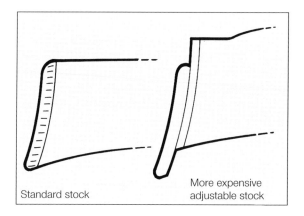

The butt is shaped to configure with the shoulder pocket.

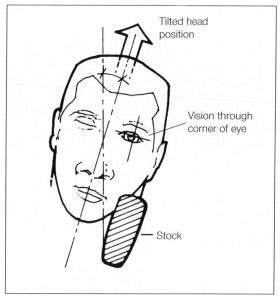

Incorrect head position.

the pulse and breathing, which are transmitted to the rifle through the shoulder.

When placing the butt into the shoulder, full contact between the butt and the shoulder should occur. The contact should be firm, but do not push the butt with too much force. Remember the importance of keeping things relaxed. This is totally different from a bullet gun, which is held very firmly into the shoulder, since a firm hold does not upset a bullet gun and is essential for weapons with a big kick.

Head

A lot of shooters bend their head to look down the sights of their rifle, but this is not good technique. The head needs to be as upright as possible with the cheek resting lightly against the cheekpiece of the stock. With the head erect and the eye placed directly behind the rear portion of the sighting mechanism, vision occurs through the centre of the eye, which allows the muscles around the eye to be relaxed. When the head is bent over the rifle, vision occurs through the top or the corner of the eye, which places strain on the eye muscles and leads to blurred vision.

The position of the cheek upon the stock is known as the stock weld. This must be the same every time the rifle is brought to the firing position as the slightest change in the stock weld will have an effect upon the pellet's point of impact. If the stock weld varies from shot to shot, you will see inconsistencies in your accuracy, with pellets being sprayed all over the target.

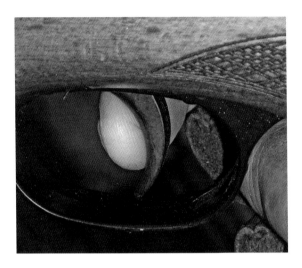

The pad of the finger (not the joint) is the area that should engage the trigger.

Firing Hand

This is the hand that operates the trigger. The positioning of this hand depends on the type of stock used. There are three types of stock: the conventional stock, the thumb-hole stock and the pistol-grip stock.

On a conventionally designed stock, you see a gradual slope that moves away from the rifle and down behind the trigger. This sloping portion of the stock, referred to as the small of the stock, is the area that provides the grip for the firing hand. The index finger down to the little finger wrap around the front of the small of the stock in a relaxed

manner, exerting a moderate amount of pressure to keep the rifle located in the shoulder pocket. The thumb goes over the top of the small of the stock, almost creating a right angle between the thumb and the trigger finger. The trigger finger itself lies alongside the trigger guard until the very moment you are ready to fire, at which point you place the pad of the trigger finger upon the trigger.

Many shooters place the crook (or joint) of the finger upon the trigger, but this is not a good technique as the mechanical movement of the finger when the crook is used is in a

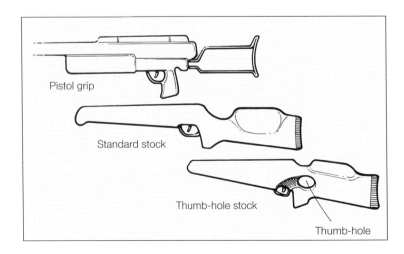

Pistol grip

Standard stock

Thumb-hole stock

Thumb-hole

There are three types of stock.

rearwards and sideways direction. The sideways movement has the effect of nudging the rifle fractionally off line. When the pad of the finger is used the movement is straight back, which of course means that the rifle is not pulled off line.

With a thumb-hole stock, you place your thumb through the hole and wrap your lower three fingers around the part of the stock directly in front of the thumb-hole.

A pistol-grip stock is the type found on most military rifles. It is basically the kind of grip you would find on a pistol but integrated into a rifle stock. The thumb wraps around the back of the pistol grip and down the inside, while the lower three fingers go down the outside of the grip and wrap around the front.

Non-Firing Hand

This hand has just one function: to support the rifle. It does this by taking up different positions, usually on the fore-end of the stock. The position of the hand is dictated by the stance taken. It is very important to keep the arm of the non-firing hand as relaxed as possible because the more muscular tension exhibited by this arm the greater the degree of wobble you will experience. The arm is kept relaxed by not squeezing the forestock, by not over-reaching, by supporting the arm, and by not holding a firing position for too long. The longer you hold a position, the greater the level of fatigue, which leads to increased tension and increased wobble.

The Prone Position (Lying Down)

When out in the field or around the farmyard, the first thing that you have to do before taking a prone position is examine the ground that you intend to lie upon, making sure that there is nothing unpleasant or even dangerous beneath you (animal droppings, broken glass, etc). Not all airgun hunting is done in

An assisted prone position. (Notice how the non-firing hand supports the stock.)

the beautiful British countryside. Quite a lot takes place on rubbish tips, in farmyards and on industrial sites. It is surprising how many hunters in the heat of the moment just drop down, without even the quickest glance to see what is on the ground they are in such a hurry to lie on!

There is absolutely no reason why the shooter should rush to take up the prone position; slow movements are quieter, and they also tend to be less obvious to the quarry. Air rifle hunting is not akin to the fast-draw antics of the Wild West; it is more like the slow deliberate style of the army sniper, where every action is pre-planned and carefully implemented. So scan the ground before you

An assisted prone position using a Polecat tripod. (Note how the elbow is used to lock the body position.)

go down, not forgetting to look for twigs that will snap when your body weight comes upon them, scaring every rabbit in the vicinity back to the safety of its burrow. Watch a fox or even a dog when it is hunting: notice, when it lies down to move those last few yards, how slowly it lowers its body like a slow-motion film. That is what you need to imitate.

The next thing to consider is the alignment of the rifle. Position it so that it is in a direct, natural line to the intended target, so that no muscular tension needs to be employed to keep the rifle fixed on that target, which requires not only that the rifle be in the correct position, but also that the body be placed directly behind it. This is the prone position used by the military. Airgun target shooters like to have the body at a 20-degree angle to the rifle,

which they believe reduces the level of muscular tension in the neck and spine.

I prefer the military-type prone position, but if you find that having your body at a 20-degree angle is more comfortable for you then adopt it, but do not exceed a 20-degree angle or you will create serious levels of muscular tension in your body. As I stated earlier, shooting is all about staying relaxed; tension is the shooter's enemy. Angles in excess of 20 degrees will also prevent you from achieving an acceptable stock weld.

To check that the rifle is on the correct natural point of aim, place your cheek against the stock to form the correct stock weld. Look through the scope then look away, moving the eyes only, not the head, at the same time taking a respiratory pause. As you look away

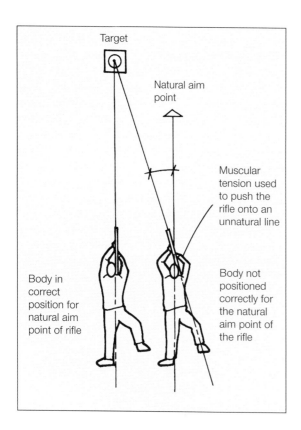

Alignment of the rifle.

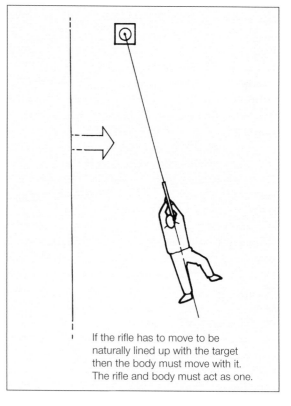

Moving body into correct position for natural aim point of rifle.

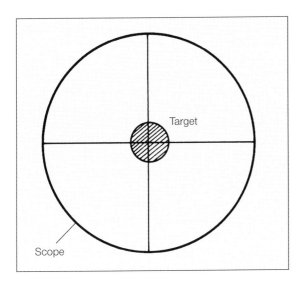

Target framed by scope.

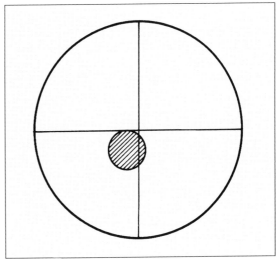

Target not framed by scope.

and take a respiratory pause you need to relax the body, which will allow the rifle to drift to its natural point of aim. When this is done look back down the scope. If the scope is framing the target, the rifle's natural point of aim is correct; if it is not then readjust the rifle's and your body position. The rifle and your body must act as one integrated unit, you cannot move the one without the other.

If the natural point of aim is incorrect, do not correct the situation by moving the rifle onto the target by itself without a corresponding body movement. Holding the rifle away from its natural aim point requires muscular resistance to be exerted against the rifle. When you pull the trigger there will be a split second of muscular relaxation, at which point the rifle will move towards its natural point of aim. Because this movement occurs just before the pellet begins to charge down the barrel, the rifle is in motion as the pellet exits the muzzle bringing about a displaced shot. Adjusting the rifle and body as a single in-tune unit, rechecking and readjusting as necessary, the shooter is able to achieve a correct alignment with the rifle's natural point of aim.

You might think that all this checking and readjusting will take up far too much time,

but that is not the case at all. A minute or so should suffice, and since air rifle shooting is not all about speed – it's about the precise placement of a very small projectile in a very small target area – then it will be time well spent.

In the prone position the front end of the stock needs to rest upon something: a log, a mound of earth, a rock or such like. With a spring-powered rifle the sand sock must be between the stock and the supporting object. If the rifle is fitted with a bipod then that will obviously provide the necessary support. (The advantage of the bipod is that it is always there when you need it, whereas you cannot always rely on rocks and logs etc.)

The non-firing arm folds back at the elbow, the hand forming a clenched fist which goes under the butt end of the stock. By tensing or relaxing the fist you can raise or lower the height of the butt, which fractionally raises or lowers the cross-hairs. The firing arm has the elbow out to the side in a position that is natural, not forced, which will provide good stability for the upper body. The leg on the non-firing side is kept straight; the leg on the firing side is bent, locking out the body to prevent side-to-side movement.

The prone position is not something that you drop into when you happen upon your quarry. It is a position you take prior to engaging your quarry, then crawl into place. We shall look at how to achieve this in the section on fieldcraft.

The Kneeling Position

As with every other firing position, the first thing to do is to try to find something that your rifle can rest upon. That object, whatever it is, will have to be just the right height. If it's too high or too low you will be forcing the rifle off its natural point of aim, using muscle resistance to do so, which is not desirable. The object that you choose to support the rifle will have to be about the same height as your shoulder when you are in the kneeling position.

In the kneeling position, the leading leg is the one on the same side as the non-firing

An unassisted kneeling position where the forearm is used to support the weapon rather than the elbow.

hand. The leg is bent at the knee, with the foot placed flat on the ground and pointing in the same direction as the rifle. The rear leg is the one on the same side as the firing hand, positioned at a right angle to the leading leg with the knee on the floor and the foot supported on the toes. The buttocks then rest on the heel of the rear foot. The torso and head are kept erect and relaxed, the rifle going into the shoulder as normal. If the rifle is rested upon an object, then the non-firing hand can come back to support the butt, as in the prone position. But if there is nothing to rest the rifle upon then the forearm, not the elbow, of the non-firing arm can rest on the thigh of the leading leg. The hand makes a cradle to support the rifle. If the elbow is rested on the leading leg, the point of contact is smaller than when the forearm is used; consequently a less stable contact is produced.

If there is a wall or tree trunk to lean my back up against, I prefer to use a crouching position instead of a kneeling one. This allows me to provide support to both firing and non-firing arms. You should practise dropping into the kneeling position on a regular basis, so that it becomes a smooth movement that you can execute the instant you spot your quarry. But do not rush this movement, as rapid movement tends to attract your quarry's attention. It needs to be a slow, controlled movement which takes a fair degree of balance, which is why the practice is necessary.

The Standing Position

This is the most challenging position to take. The problem is that it provides the least stable platform of all the firing positions, thus it produces the most wobble. This means that even the most experienced shooters will only adopt this position as a last resort.

Of course if you can find something the correct height (shoulder level) to support the rifle, you can use it to turn the standing position into a stable, accurate platform. Unfortunately this is not always possible, but if you took a tripod along with you, then a supported standing shot is always available. It is a

The crouching position which allows you to support both arms. It is also worth observing in this photo how effective the Jack Pyke camouflage is inside farm buildings.

lot easier and quicker to adopt than the kneeling position, so the quarry is less likely to be alerted.

You place the tripod about an arm's length away from your body, and rest the rifle in the yoke. Place the leading leg (the one on the same side as the non-firing hand) slightly forward with the toes pointing in the same direction as the rifle. The rifle comes to the shoulder as normal, the non-firing hand holding the tripod just below the yoke.

If no support is available, the non-supported standing position is adopted by placing the leading foot slightly forward of the body. The rifle is brought to the shoulder as normal with the non-firing hand providing support to the forestock. Some shooters rest the elbow on the hip, or on a thick army-type belt. This helps to give stability to the position and is a technique you should try to master.

A very slight bend in the knees will also help to bring stability. You have probably seen the martial arts films on the TV where

the practitioner bends at the knees; this is because he is creating a stable body position from which to repel or launch attacks. Likewise, a slight dip in the shooter's knees stabilizes the body, hence the pistol shooter dropping at the knees just prior to the discharge of his first round.

Personally, I would never use an unassisted standing position for taking quarry; it is just too unstable. If I am shooting across open fields, I always take a tripod with me for standing shots. When around farmyards there is always something around to rest the rifle upon.

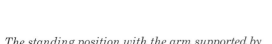

The standing position with the arm supported by the elbow in the belt – not my favourite position but it has its uses.

Practising Positions

It is imperative that you practise each of these firing positions described in this section over and over again on your range until they become second nature, and your body has the required suppleness to adopt the positions with ease. Just as a boxer hones his craft by practising each individual element – the hook, the jab, the uppercut – until he is a rounded fighter with a bag full of tools at his disposal, the shooter must practise each individual element of his sport until he too is a rounded sportsman fully equipped for a day's shooting.

The firing positions are the key to good shooting, providing a stable platform is fundamental to success. Put the work in on your foundations and everything else will just fall into place. Someone with a dirt-cheap rifle who has taken the time and invested the energy into perfecting their firing positions, will always outshoot the man with a top of the range rifle whose firing positions lack form. Remember that marksmanship is a perishable skill that needs to practised often if it is to be retained.

The Seated Position

This position is used with a tripod. You sit and bend the leading leg (the one on the same side as the non-firing hand) at the knee, bringing the heel of the foot back until it is almost under the buttock. The knee points forward in the same direction as the rifle. The rear leg, the one on the side of the firing hand, is placed almost at a right angle to the leading leg, the knee raised and the sole of the foot rested flat on the ground. The elbow of the firing arm rests on the knee, the rifle is set in the shoulder as normal with the forestock resting in the yoke of the tripod, which is set up a few feet in front of the body. The non-firing hand holds the tripod just below the yoke.

Breathing

Breath control is vital to the aiming process. If the hunter breathes while trying to aim, the rise and fall of his chest, produced by the movement of the diaphragm, will cause the rifle to move. The hunter must therefore breathe whilst carrying out sight alignment, and complete the aiming process holding his breath.

To accomplish this he inhales normally, exhales normally, then at the point when he would take the next breath he takes a respiratory pause – he holds his breath. Between breaths there is a natural momentary pause. The hunter should aim to time his cessation of breath with that pause: the muscles relax during the pause so holding the breath at this point avoids strain on the diaphragm.

Once you have assumed your firing position, breathe naturally until the hold begins to settle. (This does not happen instantly; it takes the muscles a few seconds to relax into the position you have adopted.) When settled and you are comfortable and ready for the shot, the rifle's alignment is correct, and you feel confident in success: breathe in, breathe out, before taking the next breath; in that moment between exhalation and inhalation, cease breathing. The moment breathing stops make the final adjustments to the rifle's alignment, bring the cross-hairs bang on target, then gently squeeze the trigger. Once the rifle has discharged, resume breathing.

The respiratory pause should last no more than eight to ten seconds, any longer and the average person begins to suffer from oxygen deficiency. In response, the body sends out signals telling the lungs to breathe again. These signals produce involuntary movements in the diaphragm, which interfere significantly with the shooter's ability to maintain a stable firing position.

If you have held your breath for too long, your ability to concentrate will also be affected; concentration is vital to achieving an accurate shot. If you have not managed to line the cross-hairs up with the target during the eight to ten seconds, do not be tempted to rush the shot toward the end of the pause. Instead hold the shot, go back to normal breathing, then take another respiratory pause when you feel comfortable to do so. Rushing a shot in the dying moments of the respiratory pause, when the body is beginning to feel uncomfortable, will not yield good results. A good shooter is a patient shooter, who only takes a shot when everything is almost perfect.

Trigger Control

Trigger control is one of the fundamental skills of marksmanship; an awful lot of shooters do not take the time to master it and as a result they never achieve the results they are after. The American military's sniper training school defines trigger control as:

> Causing the rifle to discharge when the sight picture is at its very best, without causing the rifle to move.

Correct trigger control is when the hunter places his trigger finger as low as possible on the trigger blade, while leaving space between the bottom of the finger and the trigger. This positioning of the finger gives the maximum mechanical advantage. In other words, pulling the trigger is easiest if the finger is positioned low. The easier the trigger is to pull, the less effort you are required to exert, and the less disturbance you create.

It is important that the pad of the trigger finger (rather than the joint) is placed on the trigger blade, so that the pull is straight back and not sideways. When the trigger is squeezed you should be able to see daylight between the top of the finger and the stock. If the trigger finger is touching the base of the stock when the trigger is squeezed, the movement of the finger will be transferred to the entire rifle instead of being isolated to the trigger blade.

With a two-stage trigger there are two distinct movements as the trigger is squeezed. The purpose is to give a smoother and mechanically less demanding pull than offered by the single-stage trigger, which just has the one movement.

With a two-stage trigger, which is found on most medium-range guns and all top-range guns, there is slack in the trigger movement. If you cock and load the weapon and point it down the range, then squeeze the trigger gently, you will notice that it moves freely. At first no resistance whatsoever is offered, then you suddenly hit resistance. The free movement phase is known as slack.

Line up your rifle with the target, assuming good stock weld and steady position, get the cross-hairs lined up on the target, then take your respiratory pause. At the same time place the finger on the trigger, taking up the slack to the point where resistance is felt. As long as the cross-hairs stay aligned with the target, you increase the tension on the trigger until the sear is released, causing the weapon to discharge.

If the cross-hairs move off the target during the taking up of the slack, do not apply any more tension to the trigger, but pause until the cross-hairs are back on the target. Then, if your firing position is still free of tension and your respiratory pause is still comfortable, continue to squeeze the trigger. If the respiratory pause is strained, then do not try to rush the shot, just release your hold slowly on the trigger and start again.

You will by now have realized that you do not just grasp the trigger and pull. Handling the trigger properly requires a very controlled squeeze that is coordinated with the respiratory pause. A young lad who was having trouble with his shooting asked me if I would be able to help him. I agreed and went to watch him shoot. His pellets were being thrown all over the target, no two landing in the same place. His problem was simple: he was yanking the trigger; there was simply no control or coordination in his trigger pull. Once I got him to position his finger correctly, and squeeze rather than yank, whilst coordinating the squeeze with a respiratory pause, he started knocking up some very tight groupings and was soon on to the centre of his target. So remember that exercising proper trigger control is a key requirement of successful marksmanship.

Follow-Through

We have covered all the fundamentals of marksmanship, but there is one additional and more advanced skill that is worth learning because it increases your chances still further of making a clean kill with the first shot. This is follow-through, termed such because it involves continuing to apply all the fundamental skills described above both as the weapon fires and immediately after it fires. That sounds a little confusing so let me explain. Follow-through consists of:

• Keeping the head in firm contact with the stock, thus maintaining the stock weld as the weapon discharges, and continuing to do so for a second or two after the pellet has left the barrel.
• Keeping the finger on the trigger all the way to the rear, not releasing until several seconds after the pellet has left the barrel. The aim is not to release the trigger until the recoil has come to a complete halt.

• Continuing to look through the scope until a few seconds after the pellet has left the barrel. When doing this you will quite often actually see the pellet powering along through the scope and see it strike the quarry.
• Ensuring the muscles stay relaxed until a few seconds after the pellet has left the barrel.
• Not reacting to the weapon's recoil by pulling away from it or tensing up as the weapon pushes into your shoulder. Do not react to the noise caused by the muzzle blast by flinching.

Good follow-through ensures that the weapon is allowed to fire and recoil naturally, so that the hunter and the rifle operate as a single unit.

Assisted shooting position using the roof of a Land Rover for support.

Assisted standing position.

CHAPTER TWO

Suitable Weapons

It was obvious when I first began this project that in order for the book to be complete it would have to include a chapter on weapons. But the question that faced me was which weapons should I include?

During my research I discovered that some companies sell air weapons as a sideline, importing one or two models from abroad. Such companies have no technical backup to provide advice or spares for those looking to repair a weapon, so I decided to look elsewhere.

After much careful consideration and a lot more research, I decided that the company that could work with me on this project was BSA (Birmingham Small Arms). With over a hundred years of uninterrupted airgun production, this British company manufactures many components, including the barrel, in their extensive Birmingham factory. The company is respected worldwide for its gunsmithing skills and innovation, making rifles that can perform in the most extreme conditions the world has to offer. To my knowledge at least one Arctic expedition equipped itself with BSA bullet rifles, putting their lives in the hands of these firearms because they knew they would operate when required, despite the extreme conditions that the Arctic throws at man and his equipment.

You may consider the example of the Arctic a bit irrelevant as regards airgun hunting, but you will soon discover when you take to the hunting field in the British countryside, especially in the north, that our climate can certainly test weaponry. There is the cold then the rain, which can cause severe rust to a gun

both externally and internally. On top of this there is the mud, the muck, and the wind, which carries particles of dirt. If you are near the sea, as I am, the air is heavily laden with salt, which can rust through metal in the blink of an eye.

We must also not forget all the knocks and scrapes our rifle must endure on a day's hunting, so you can see that to be any use in the field, and to survive the beating it will receive week in week out, a rifle must be as hard as nails. Many rifles fall flat at this first hurdle; this is because not enough thought is put into a rifle's toughness. Manufacturers seem to be obsessed with accuracy and looks, sometimes to the detriment of all else. Do not judge a gun for a moment on what it looks like: looks are an irrelevance as far as hunting performance goes.

What you need to know, and what nobody seems to tell you, is how tough the gun is. Will it still work if you drop it? If it gets soaked will it fail to operate? If you happen to neglect it, will it rust away? Can it cope with dirty conditions? These are the questions you need to ask. What good is a supremely accurate gun to anybody if it cannot endure seriously rough field conditions. How, then, can you determine if a gun is tough and durable?

Research: lots and lots of it. Study magazines, look in books, ask at gun shops, gun clubs and anywhere else you come across airgun shooters. Manufacturers' glossy brochures tell you next to nothing apart from technical specs. It is personal testimony that you need to seek out. Only those who have used and abused a weapon in the field can tell you how it copes with the rugged treatment. Price is no indicator of how tough a weapon is.

I remember testing a gun that cost just short of £700. On the very first hunting trip with it I happened to knock the safety catch on a concrete column in a cattle shed. It wasn't a very severe blow at all but, to my utter disbelief, the safety catch sheared clean off. You would have thought that something that expensive would have been able to take the rough with the smooth. Alas, no.

On the other hand, I have a BSA Meteor, which is a basic standard spring-gun. It has been bashed, dropped and neglected, and it is still in full working order. Some of the toughest guns on the market are some of the simplest. It stands to reason that the more working parts in a rifle's construction, the greater the scope for things to go wrong. This is one of the main reasons why so many professional pest controllers opt for a basic break-barrel, spring-powered air weapon.

PARTS AND CHARACTERISTICS

The Magazine

A multi-shot PCP has a rotating magazine that delivers the pellets to the barrel, in response to the movement of a bolt or lever action. On a lot of PCPs the magazine protrudes from the block, the waiting pellets are completely exposed to the environment in which you are shooting.

I remember using a PCP with this model of magazine in a grain storage shed, making the air rich with grain dust. My quarry was the feral pigeons filling the rafters. After only a few minutes in that environment, the pellets in the magazine looked like cake decorations sprinkled in sugar icing; the grain dust had settled heavily upon them. BSA have their own patented magazine design, which sees the magazine completely housed within the block. Consequently, the waiting pellets are fully protected against contamination from

the dust and dirt existing in the environment in which you are operating in. To my mind this provides the better model for the hunter and pest controller. A magazine that protrudes from the block is also subject to damage.

Whilst using a PCP with a protruding magazine that stuck out of the bottom of the block, I happened to slip on a muddy bank. As I fell with a heavy thud onto my buttocks, the rifle and I parted company. The gun ended up in some rocks, I came to a halt just short of a very nasty looking patch of nettles. When I retrieved the rifle I noticed that a chunk of metal had been taken out of the magazine. This could not have happened to the type of magazine used by BSA as it is totally enclosed within the block.

If you intend to do some night shooting, then you need to consider the fact that you will be removing and replacing the magazine in thick darkness, with little more than a torch to guide your movements. The magazine therefore, needs to be of a design that is easy to remove and replace, it should include some features that ensure it cannot be loaded upside down or back to front. BSA magazines are designed in such a fashion that they can only go into the block in one way. There is a small probe on the right-hand side of the magazine, so that even in pitch darkness you can by touch alone insert the magazine correctly.

The BSA magazine.

Loading a BSA Magazine

Whilst looking at the BSA patented magazine, we might as well take a look at how to load it.

Take a look at the pellet tin and make sure that you have the right calibre and type of pellet for your rifle. This may sound obvious but you would be surprised how often the wrong pellet is selected.

Hold the magazine between your finger and thumb with the cover plate screw facing you, this will ensure that the pellets go in the right way round.

Push the pellet nose into the vacant loading chamber and press it down, so that the pellet's skirt is just below the magazine's cover plate.

Rotate the central body of the magazine anti-clockwise with your finger and thumb, till the next vacant loading chamber lines up with the hole in the cover plate. Insert another pellet and repeat the process till the magazine is full; at which point a white dot will appear on the top of the magazine's body. When this dot appears you will have ten pellets loaded.

During the loading process, the magazine's main body can, if necessary, be moved back by one position. Press the escapement mechanism on the bottom left-hand side of the magazine.

If you should happen to load a pellet into the loading chamber the wrong way round, skirt first, do not worry. Place a thin object, like a jeweller's screwdriver, into the skirt of the pellet and push it out.

The Barrel

A lot of shooters are seduced by a good-looking stock, but they pay scant attention to a much more important facet of a rifle, the barrel. The barrel is perhaps the single most important part of the rifle. A good shooter can compensate for a poor trigger or poor stock design, but nothing can be done to compensate for a poorly crafted barrel. So what makes for a good barrel? To explain this you will first need to know something about the anatomy of a barrel.

The barrel is a precision piece of engineering. It is subject to very fine and accurate measurements during the process of manufacture, which only a skilled machine operator can achieve.

When guns were first invented the barrel was simply a smooth tube down which the projectile travelled. Then a Swiss gentleman came up with the idea of cutting longitudinal grooves into the inner surface of the barrel, improving the accuracy of the rifle. Not long after that an unknown genius gave the grooves a slight twist, thus inventing the rifled barrel.

The spiral grooving inside the barrel causes the projectile to spin as it travels down the barrel, giving it gyroscopic stability during flight. The projectile rotates around an axis (the axis is an imaginary line drawn through the centre of the projectile) distributing the rotation equally on both sides of the axis. Put simply, the rotation of the projectile gives it the characteristics necessary for balanced flight through the air. Knowledge as to the value of rotation is in itself quite ancient. Going back to a time before the invention of guns, archers and javelin throwers used to cause their missiles to spin in flight. The stability this gave increased the accuracy and range of the missile. Without the gyroscopic stability produced by rifling, the projectile would not be able to fly headfirst but would go end over end.

When a pellet travels down a barrel it rotates around its axis. If however, the pellet was not placed concentrically within the bore (if the centre of the pellet's mass is not in line with the centre of the bore), the pellet will rotate unevenly and spiral out of control upon exiting the muzzle.

A badly centred pellet in the bore will happen if the ammunition is poorly manufactured, which results in it being unbalanced. Or the shooter has rushed, not centralizing the pellet correctly by pushing it to one side or the other. (This of course only occurs in springers and single-shot PCPs. A magazine-fed PCP centralizes the pellet mechanically, but problems can occur if the pellets are not loaded correctly into the magazine, or if the feeding probe becomes damaged.)

When a pellet is pushed gently into the breech of an air rifle, the head of the pellet engages the rifling and centralizes itself within the bore. This only occurs when the pellet is placed carefully into the breech; rough handling can cause the head to veer off-centre, causing the pellet to spiral out of control upon exiting the muzzle. So take care when loading. It is the basic operation of taking care that can make or break a shot.

The twist rate of the barrel (the amount of rotation the rifling gives to the pellet) is absolutely crucial, too much and the pellet exiting the muzzle will spin hopelessly out of control, too little and the pellet will not have sufficient stabilization.

Every model of gun requires the rifling to correspond specifically to its design, significantly the length and type of ammunition

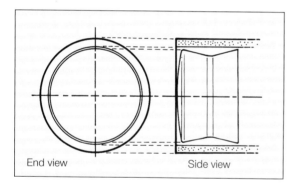

Pellet correctly centralized in bore.

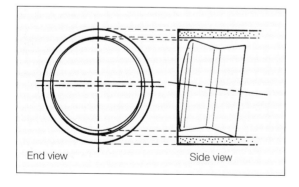

Pellet incorrectly centralized in bore.

used. The average twist rate for a good airgun (.17 or .22) is roughly one twist in ½in (13mm). This means that when the pellet has travelled 17½in (44.5cm) down the barrel, it will have rotated 360 degrees through its axial centre: it will have made one complete turn.

Nearly all air rifle barrels are chocked at the muzzle. A choke is a very minimal constriction of the barrel at the muzzle, the constriction covering approximately 10 per cent of the barrel's length. The choke compresses the pellet, an action known as chocking, this traps the air behind the pellet giving it an extra boost. The choke has to be extremely well engineered, as it has a major influence on a weapon's accuracy. A barrel is not square at the muzzle end, it has a concave shape. Crowning is the term used to describe the giving of this shape to the barrel.

The manufacturing of a barrel is a skilled undertaking, which must be done to a high standard or the rifle will be next to useless. It is essential that this is understood.

The following extract from BSA's publicity material shows you why their barrels are among the best in the world.

'The barrel of an air rifle has even more of an influence on accuracy than many shooters realize. Not only must a barrel be expertly made, with precision rifling, a properly finished bore and a perfectly true crown at the muzzle, the entire barrel setup must be compatible with the rifle it's fitted to and the pellets used in it. For all of these factors to come together for every rifle, total control over barrel production is required. That is why BSA always makes its own barrels. Our unmatched experience in airgun making has proven that the degree of control we insist on is absolutely essential for top performance. At BSA, we control every process that goes into the making of a barrel, from the initial selection of the steel blanks, through the forming of the bore and its rifling, all the way to the final finishing. We know that every one of these processes has a significant effect on the performance of a barrel and that is another reason why we maintain control of them. Our barrels are not only designed and made by us to our exclusive specifications, their configuration is unique to BSA.'

Not all airgun manufacturers make their own barrels, BSA is fairly unique in this respect, hence their barrels are so good. A number of manufacturers use a Walther barrel which is another name that can be trusted.

The Stock

Before you can assess the qualities of the stock, you need to become familiar with the various parts.

The stock is the juncture that allows man and rifle to come together as one. In order to facilitate this union the stock must fit to the individual characteristics of your body as well as possible. Some of us have long arms some short, some have broad shoulders others narrow, some have long necks others short. So what fits one shooter perfectly well may be a horrible fit for another.

One of the first things that is done for a sniper in the American military, is to have him measured for a stock; which is then custom built to marry perfectly with the contours of his body. This is considered a fundamental prerequisite for advanced standards of marksmanship.

With regards to standard stocks, the only way to see how they fit is to go to the gun shop and try them up against your shoulder. All

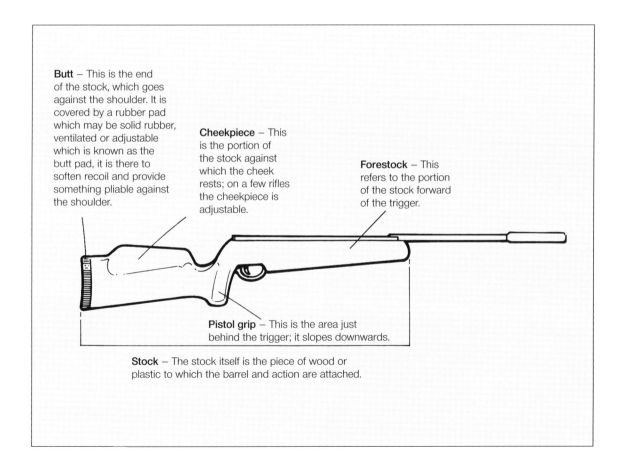

Butt – This is the end of the stock, which goes against the shoulder. It is covered by a rubber pad which may be solid rubber, ventilated or adjustable which is known as the butt pad, it is there to soften recoil and provide something pliable against the shoulder.

Cheekpiece – This is the portion of the stock against which the cheek rests; on a few rifles the cheekpiece is adjustable.

Forestock – This refers to the portion of the stock forward of the trigger.

Pistol grip – This is the area just behind the trigger; it slopes downwards.

Stock – The stock itself is the piece of wood or plastic to which the barrel and action are attached.

The stock and its parts.

standard stocks will of course be something of a compromise because they are designed around the average man, and there is, of course, no such thing as an average man.

When choosing a stock do not be swayed by appearance or cost; you are far better off going for a cheap stock that fits your shoulder well, than a beautiful piece of wood that feels uncomfortable. I am presently restoring an antiquated weapon that was, in its day, a cheap and cheerful type of gun. But it has one of the best fitting stocks I have ever come across. Do not think that price is any indicator of how a stock will fit against your shoulder.

As mentioned earlier in this book, there are three main stock types; the standard sporting stock, the thumb-hole stock and the pistol-grip stock. But is any one of these better suited to hunting than the other? Not really, it all comes down to personal choice. Whichever feels most comfortable against your shoulder is the best one for you.

There is, however, a feature I consider to be indispensable no matter what the stock type, and that is some kind of grip on the forestock and around the pistol grip. This ensures that the stock offers purchase in slippery conditions.

As a hunter or pest controller you will gain plenty of experience of slippery conditions.

Your hands will get wet, muddy and bloody. Where there are large numbers of cattle they may also get covered in muck. Shooting, especially around farmyards, is a dirty business. Combine this with heavy rainfall and your rifle will become very slippery indeed. If there is no form of grip on the stock, you'll have no more hope of holding on to it than you would a bar of soap in the shower.

The criss-cross pattern (chequering) that you see cut into the wood of the stock on some rifles is not for decoration. It roughens the surface of the stock to give gripping surfaces to the palm of the trigger hand, and the fingers of the support hand. As a hunter, you need this feature on your rifle in the same way that you need grip on your car tyres. For serious hunting, I would not even consider a rifle that did not posses this feature.

Some rifles are set in a synthetic stock: which is made from a man-made substance. On the BSA XL Tactical, it is a high-impact polymer compound. Many of these man-made stocks, are formed out of a material that has a roughened surface to provide maximum grip, thus performing admirably well in wet and slippery conditions.

Synthetic stocks are very anti-abrasive and will not scratch as easily as their wooden counterparts. Another feature offered by the

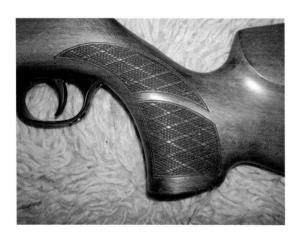

An example of quality chequering: a standard feature on all BSA rifles.

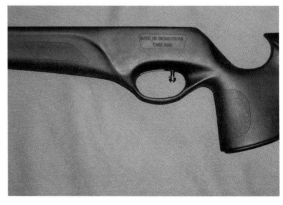

The grip on a synthetic stock may not look as impressive as the chequering on a wooden stock but it is very effective.

synthetic stock is its total weather resistance. No amount of moisture can induce them to warp. Unfortunately, the same cannot be said for wooden stocks which can and do warp.

The synthetic stock is far easier to care for than the wooden type. A wooden stock needs to be oiled on a regular basis. Whereas, you don't have to do a single thing to the synthetic in the way of maintenance, it will remain durable even if totally neglected. This factor makes them a firm favourite among pest controllers.

Wooden stocks can have an oiled or a varnished finish. Oiling is done in the factory, a coat of warm oil is applied to the raw wood and left to dry for a week. The varnished stock is less common, but in the field it provides a tougher finish. Should it become damaged however, the only way to repair it is to strip and re-varnish the entire stock. The oiled stock, simply needs fresh oil applied to the damaged area. Stocks can also have a paint finish, which in my opinion provides the toughest finish of all. It is not a standard factory feature but a customized finish.

Scope Rail

The scope rail is a block of metal specifically designed to fasten to the top of the rifle, providing a receiving point onto which the scopes can be attached. On a spring-powered rifle, the scope rail sits on top of the cylinder and on a PCP it sits on top of the block. I believe that a scope rail is an essential feature for a hunting rifle that has to operate in the field, the scope having to take all sorts of knocks and bangs. To survive such treatment it needs to be incredibly well anchored to the rifle, the best way to achieve this is to have a scope rail.

Lots of spring-powered rifles have grooves cut into the top of the cylinder, these grooves are simply not in the same league as a scope rail as they offer a shallower purchase and can wear down over a period of time. Because of the violent recoil produced by spring-powered guns, the scope needs a very secure fixing to the rifle to stop what is called creep, the gradual movement of the scope which will knock it off

zero. The scope can be more securely fastened to a rail than it can to grooves, giving greater resistance to creep.

A rail on a spring-powered weapon can be dampened, that is to say there can be an energy-absorbing material between the scope rail and the cylinder which will dampen the effects of the recoil being transmitted to the scope. A non-dampened scope rail on a spring-powered gun could be compared to being hit in the chest with a clenched fist: it will knock you backwards and take the wind out of you. A dampened scope rail is like having a sheet of thick rubber covering your chest, which will absorb most of the impact of the fist when it strikes, resulting in only the dullest thud being felt. Thus, a scope attatched to a dampened scope rail will result in less discomfort than it would if it were attached to grooves or a non-dampened scope rail.

Safety Catch

On a hunting rifle the safety catch must not only be easily reached by the trigger finger, it must be silent in operation. It amazes me that so many rifle manufacturers go to so much trouble making a silencer for their weapon, and yet fit it with a safety catch that makes nearly as much noise as the rifle when it is discharged. A noisy safety catch can alert the attentive ear of your quarry to your presence.

I tested a very expensive PCP rifle some months ago. When I disengaged the safety catch while studying the rifle at my desk in my study, my brother heard the movement in the next room – despite the door being closed.

So when selecting a hunting rifle in the gun shop apply and disengage the safety catch a number of times to see what it sounds like.

Bear in mind that while safety catches are designed to prevent accidental discharge of the weapon, they are far from infallible. Some manufacturers even write in a gun's operating manual that the user should not consider it impossible for a gun to discharge with the safety catch applied. Wear, corrosion, or dirt, can all potentially render a safety catch ineffective, and the safety catch can also be knocked off accidentally when moving through thick undergrowth.

Cocking Mechanism

The cocking mechanism on a hunting rifle, like the safety catch, needs to operate quietly. Successful airgun hunting involves getting really close to your quarry, which requires good camouflage and silence. Therefore, the cocking mechanism on the weapon you choose must have a smooth, quiet operation; so cock it half a dozen times in the shop to test the sound. Even a spring-powered weapon when well lubricated should not make much noise during the cocking stroke. As to whether a lever action or bolt action is better on a hunting rifle it makes no odds: they are both effective so choose whichever you like.

Silencer

All PCPs need to be fitted with a silencer for hunting purposes and nearly every PCP on the market has one fitted as standard. Without a silencer a PCP is excessively noisy, possessing a booming sound. Silencers on a spring-powered weapon are a bit futile, as they only reduce the noise to a small degree, as most of the noise coming from a discharging springer relates to the movement of the spring, which of course no silencer can mitigate against.

If you intend to silence a spring-powered weapon, you should have a basic tune-up carried out on the action, this will make it run smoother and quieter. Without the tune-up, I don't see the point of a silencer on a spring-powered gun. It's just a half measure though it does make a good cocking aid, giving added leverage so that the gun can be cocked more easily.

But don't you need a silencer in order to hunt quarry? It can be an advantage but it is not essential, even the very quietest of guns fitted with a state of the art silencer emit noise, which is well within the audible receiving range of the quarry, you will be hunting so they will hear the rifle discharging. With the non-silenced weapon it is the kind of sound they make more than the volume that can cause a problem. It is a very violent sound, that has the same effect on animals as a backfiring car has on humans. Though a silenced weapon will not go undetected by quarry upon discharge, it will cause less alarm and hopefully less flight, which is an advantage when, for example shooting feral pigeons. When forty of them are roosting in the rafters of the same building you don't want the whole roost to take to the wing the second the first shot is fired, so for such shooting a good quality silencer is worth having.

The best silencers have active baffles. Baffles are blast deflecting elements made out of some soft material, like felt or foam, that absorbs noise. Spring mounted baffles have springs at the front and rear of the silencer tube, which enables the baffles to adjust themselves to provide optimum resistance according to the power and volume of the rifle's muzzle blast.

As a side note on the subject of silencers, I should let you know that the animals and birds do not always react in the way you would expect.

I was shooting a host of feral pigeons inside a barn. I was using a non-silenced spring-powered weapon that sounded more like an elephant gun than it did an air rifle. The sound of the muzzle blast was magnified to a number of decibels by the acoustics within the shed, but not a single pigeon took to flight. Yet on another almost identical occasion, using a very sophisticated PCP with a state of the art silencer that was as quiet as a whisper, the first shot which struck its target induced the entire roost to take to the wing. A couple of seconds after the first shot and not a pigeon remained. I have no explanation for this odd occurrence, it just goes to show that you cannot take anything for granted when out hunting with an air rifle.

Calibre

The calibre is the diameter of the rifle's bore, the bore is the hollow interior of the barrel which has been bored out by a special drill.

There are four calibres in which air rifles are made but we will consider only three of these. The .177 (4.5mm), .22 (5.5mm) and .25 (there is some variation here but about 6.25mm). Let me start by saying that all three calibres are effective at killing quarry, if correctly employed with a rifle of sufficient power at the suitable range for the pellet. The big swing today is towards .177 pellets. The reason for this is accuracy. A .177 pellet has a flatter trajectory than the other two calibres.

The trajectory is the arc that a pellet makes in its flight through space from the barrel to the target. If you fired a pellet in a straight line it would run out of energy long before it reached your target, being overcome by the forces of gravity. So the barrel is elevated, causing the pellet shot from rifle to target to arc. Part of the pellet's journey, when it reaches the pinnacle of the arc, is a drop. During the drop it is not utilizing its own energy to travel, just like a skier hurtling down a mountain or a car rolling down a hill with its handbrake off. It is this drop that gives the pellet the legs to reach the target.

The faster a pellet travels (the speed of the travel is referred to as its velocity and is measured in feet per second) the less of an arc from rifle to target it requires and, consequently, the less elevation you have to put on the barrel. This truer flatter line from barrel to target makes for more accurate shooting.

A .177 pellet is the fastest travelling of the three calibres due to its lighter weight, so its flatter trajectory makes it the most accurate of the three, being far more forgiving to errors. This is why it is fast becoming the calibre of choice for hunters, but personally I do not like .177. The pellets are absolutely tiny and I find them far too fiddly for my rather fat fingers.

At ranges between 30 and 35yd (27 and 32m) .22 is the largest calibre that you can employ; and though they have a much steeper trajectory than a .177, they can still produce very accurate results when used properly, though they are a harder pellet to use than a .177. The .22 may be only 1mm bigger than the .177, but that 1mm makes a lot of difference to the pellet's size. The .22 is a lot easier to handle, it is also heavier than its little cousin, the .177. A .22 pellet will weigh about 14–21 grains, the featherweight .177 weighing in at around 7–8.64 grains. You can see that the .22 is generally twice the weight of the .177. As a consequence of being bigger and heavier, the .22 retains more of its energy in flight than does the .177. The table below gives some idea of the difference in energy retention between the two calibres.

You can see from the table below that the .177 loses roughly three times as much energy as the .22 over the same distance. This means that the .22 has considerably more punch when it strikes the target, this is the main reason why those who use .22 favour it. Due to its heavier hitting power, the .22 can be used to take body shots, aiming for the heart of feral pigeons. But the .177 is too light for such a shot.

The truth is that both these calibres have their merits: one is very accurate, the other hard hitting. They both do the job and it is really up to personal choice which you go for.

There is one more interesting fact that might sway your choice as regards these two

Difference in energy retention between .22 and .177 calibre weapons

Distance the pellet has travelled (yd)	Energy level of pellet (ft/lb)	
	.177 8.2 grains	**.22 21.4 grains**
10	9.26	10.37
20	7.69	9.84
30	6.38	9.12

calibres. The lighter .177 is surprisingly less affected by crosswinds than the heavier .22. The fact that the .22 is more easily blown off course probably relates to its larger surface area and slower velocity.

I have not forgotten the third calibre, the .25. This calibre is used by a very small number of people as it is erroneously believed it will not go beyond 20–25yd (18–23m). This, however, happens to be my favourite calibre because it has such a stunning knock-down effect on quarry. Literally knocking them off their feet as it thumps into their body. With the .25 you are not just limited to head shots, you can legitimately shoot birds and rats in the body, aiming for the chest cavity. Even rabbits can be taken with a body shot, though it is still best to stick to the rabbit's head as the body cavity is rather large and you need to select just the right spot or you will injure rather than kill it.

A lot of feral pigeon and rat shooting is done inside at very close range, so being able to take a body shot gives me a very large target area, which at such short ranges is next to impossible to miss. This ensures that no damage is done to the fabric of the building. I use a .25 calibre a lot and have discovered that it can be utilized to devastating effect at distances out to 30yd (27m), but due to its low velocity the pellet has a trajectory with a steep curve making it a challenge for the shooter's markmanship. (The flatter the trajectory the easier it is to achieve accuracy and the .25 has the steepest trajectory of all the calibres.)

Of course you could keep a number of weapons in different calibres, therefore giving yourself a variety of options which would enable you to select the calibre best suited to the particular type of shooting you are doing on a given day.

I keep guns in all three calibres. These need not be expensive. My main weapon was reasonably expensive but several of the others were acquired secondhand, in a rather sorry state which I restored to health, giving me an armoury of weapons for not too much money.

Power

How much power does a hunting air rifle need to possess?

The maximum power rating that a non-FAC air rifle can posses is 12ft per lb, which is more than sufficient to kill all the relevant quarry species up to 30yd (27m). But most sporting rifles have a power rating of 11½ft per lb, simply because airguns can vary their power output and can, over a period of time, actually increase in power. If rifles were therefore manufactured right up to the legal limit of 12ft per lb, even the slightest increase in power would nudge them over the legal limit and put you in possession of an illegal weapon, a crime that carries the penalty of a severe jail sentence. So manufacturers sensibly manufacture their weapons to produce 11½ft per lb, so that there is a buffer zone should the weapon happen to increase in power.

Can you get away with less than 11½ft per lb of power for hunting quarry? Yes you can, as long as you don't expect to take any long-range shots at a range not exceeding 20yd (18m). A weapon producing a power output of 8½ft per lb will kill a rabbit if a head shot is taken at about 15yd (14m), and with weapons producing 10ft per lb, that range could be increased to about 25yd (23m). So the less powerful the weapon's capacity to kill quarry, the closer you will have to be.

BSA RIFLES ON TEST

Magazines are full of rifle reviews and the results of tests designed to assess a rifle's performance. Such tests are all very well and good but I find they don't really tell me what I most want to know: a rifle's longevity, durability and reliability. Most rifle reviews are based on only a few weeks of handling the weapon, which is no time at all to judge these factors.

I don't really want lots of technical information: what I seek to know is how well a gun performs in the field when it is soaking wet, basted in mud and bashed about. Then I want to know what happens if I should drop the weapon, which is a fairly regular occurrence for me: will it break or will it continue to work like a dream? We must not forget the question of rust: if I should happen to neglect the gun for a day or two will it rust away to nothing?

The most important question that I want answered is how well does the gun kill? I know that sounds a bit brutal, but let us not forget that a hunting rifle is a tool designed for killing, and so as a potential buyer of a weapon you need to know how well it performs its primary function.

Many rifles have the required level of power for killing, but how does that power release itself when the pellet strikes the quarry? Does it smash through bone and tissue like a sledgehammer, causing massive damage and instantaneous death? Or does it drill right through the quarry, going in one side and out the other, leaving a hole like a surgical incision which resembles a hot needle going into butter? In the latter case, unless it goes straight through brain tissue or a vital organ, it will not cause death. Whereas the sledgehammer type does not have to be so precisely delivered; its impact is spread over a larger area, inflicting greater tissue damage, creating a higher degree of blood loss, and thus more rapid onset of shock resulting in near instantaneous death.

Rifles that drill through the quarry have a degree of over-penetration; that is to say the pellet goes in one side and out the other, the exiting pellet still having sufficient shape and energy to cause damage to property, which is not something you want in a pest control setting, such as an industrial building with large amounts of glass.

Most rifle reviews don't really tackle the issues I have raised above, so for this book I decided to take four very good rifles and put them through six months of hell, up here on the north-east coast of Scotland, with the aim of testing them to and beyond their limits. During this six months I would take them into the field in all weathers, and put them through more wear and tear than most shooters would put their rifles through in three years. Basically, I have done everything I can

to make these rifles fail, I've dropped them, got them dirty, handled them roughly and given them scant amounts of care. But most of all I have examined the killing ability of these weapons to see what they are capable of doing. You will probably have noticed that air rifle manufacturers give their rifles the most inane names: the Ultra, the Lightning, the Super Ten. Why they don't give rifles a name that reflects their main purpose in life is beyond me. So, as I introduce each rifle, I shall give it a name or classification that more aptly describes its purpose.

The BSA Ultra Multi-Shot .22 Calibre

I would call this the farmyard gun. Its minuscule length gives it the appearance of a sawn-off shotgun, making it ideal for use in confined spaces where a conventional barrel is more than an inconvenience. This gun is a specialist that will more than meet the challenges of what I call the cluttered hunting environment – farmyards, certain industrial locations, overgrown woodlands, rubbish tips, and derelict buildings. All of these areas are an impediment to free movement and just as dogs are specifically bred small to work in confined spaces, the Ultra was made small to deal with cluttered hunting environments.

Since the Ultra is the expert when it comes to deployment in confined spaces, it's a firm

The compact, easy-to-handle BSA Ultra.

favourite with those who hunt rats and feral pigeons, as well as those who enjoy shooting from a hide. To my knowledge, the Ultra is the shortest gun on the market with the exception of some very unusual and expensive hand-made weapons. Most of the carbines measure in at around 35in (88cm), but the Ultra is just 32½in (82cm) long. Those few inches make an incredible amount of difference when it comes to tight spaces.

A lot of my shooting is done around farm-yards and quite a few of them resemble scrap yards, with old oil drums and bits of rusting machinery all covered in a mat of wild under-growth, and the most potent stinging nettles I have ever encountered. In places like this there is hardly room to place one foot in front of the other. So, as you can imagine, there is not a lot of room to shoulder a gun. With larger rifles I have often found it difficult, or even impossible, to shoulder the weapon in such locations.

If you look at military weapons, especially those from World War II, you will see that one of the major features of a weapon designed for use in urban warfare, where space can be tight, is shortness of barrel. The Thomson sub machine gun for example, as used by Commandos. So, if you are going to be shoot-ing in tight places then get yourself a carbine, a short rifle, like the Ultra.

The Ultra is set in a conventional wooden stock that is chequered on the forestock and around the pistol grip, which provides above-average grip even in wet conditions, making the stock viable for hunting purposes and pest control operations.

The Ultra has a unique cocking system exclusive to BSA. Most PCPs have some form of lever or bolt to operate the cocking mech-anism that when drawn back and returned will rotate the magazine, deliver a pellet to the barrel and set the trigger, all in one inte-grated movement. So when the bolt or lever is operated, the weapon is ready to be dis-charged, the only feature to prevent an acci-dental discharge being the safety catch.

The Ultra has what is termed an MMC cocking mechanism: micro-movement cocking. As suggested by MMC, only a very small move-ment is required to cock this weapon. It is cocked by depressing a plunger located at the forefront of the stock with the side of your first two fingers. This plunger does not rotate the magazine having nothing whatever to do with the ammunition feeding system. The cocking plunger just sets the trigger, nothing else.

To the rear of the block on the right-hand side there is a spring-loaded release catch. When depressed this releases a pellet-loading probe which springs backwards out of the rear of the block. When returned this pellet probe loads the next pellet in the magazine into the breech.

What BSA have done by dividing the cocking system from the pellet feed is produce a totally foolproof safety system. You can operate the pellet-loading probe to place a pellet in the breech then go off in search of your quarry. When you locate it, you are ready for action: simply depress the cocking plunger, which has a quiet, smooth action, and you are ready to fire.

All hunters walk around with a pellet up the breech ready for action, but that also means the gun is cocked, and the only thing pre-venting an accidental discharge is the safety catch, which is not foolproof. The Ultra can

Depressing the cocking plunger on the BSA Ultra.

Release catch for pellet probe

The pellet probe release catch.

be toted around with a pellet up the breech ready for action with no danger of an accidental discharge because the trigger is not set, making this the safest cocking system on the market. The safety catch is designed to allow you to move around with the weapon loaded and ready for action but it is not foolproof. The MMC on the Ultra is.

I do a lot of rabbit hunting in an old quarry in the middle of a farm. The quarry is a four-acre site covered in huge rocks, most of them covered in moss. Moving around in the quarry requires the dexterity of a mountain goat and, not being a goat, I spend as much time on my backside as I do on my feet. I like to use the Ultra simply because it is so safe. A conventional safety catch could be knocked and disengaged when I fall, but the Ultra's divided cocking mechanism and pellet feeding system make it foolproof in this kind of environment.

Now let's get down to the nitty gritty: the Ultra's killing power. The comments that follow relate to the .22 calibre Ultra, as this is the calibre that I tested. Though this gun is small it packs a really impressive punch. It has what I refer to as a full-blooded strike force, that is to say it has one heck of a knock-down ability.

Remember that just because a gun is at the legal power limit it does not mean it is the ultimate killing weapon. In this respect there are tremendous differences from one make of gun to another. A pellet fired from the Ultra smashes through the quarry's skull as it would an eggshell and ploughs into the brain doing massive tissue damage. The shot delivered by some guns is just too clean and tidy for my liking. The greater the level of damage the higher the degree of shock and the more fatal the wound. So I want a gun that literally pounds into the animal's head like a small mallet and, in this area, the Ultra delivers. It is a really effective killing machine and that is a feature that should be much more highly prized than a fancy stock.

The Ultra comes fitted with a silencer, which makes it a reasonably quiet weapon. I wouldn't refer to it as silent nor would I call it noisy. Like most PCPs it emits a puff kind of sound when the pellet exits the muzzle, which though well within the audible range of the quarry species is not the kind of noise that causes undue alarm.

The metal on the Ultra is blued in the Birmingham factory and as long as you keep it well wiped down with the correct oil on a regular basis, it will resist rust tolerably well, but neglect it and the rust will soon break through, especially if left soaking wet. The breech-block is not blued; it is anodized so is impervious to rust no matter how hard it tries to take hold. As to ruggedness, the Ultra is a very well put together little rifle, the individual parts being substantial robust pieces of machined metal.

I have hammered one of these little rifles for six months solid and have on several occasions dropped it. Nothing ever seems to break, and despite the fact that I have managed to scratch both stock and barrel the little gun comes up nice and shiny after a quick refresh with specialist oils.

I'd describe it as a very durable little gun, and I think the MMC system makes for an extremely reliable action that should last for many years without throwing up any problems. This is the sort of action that should go through 100,000 pellets or more without missing a stroke.

The Ultra is a very easy little gun to use. I used the one I had on test to teach a young lad how to shoot; he found the gun very light and manoeuvrable and, though I let him use a number of far more expensive PCPs, he always wanted to return to the Ultra, stating that it was the most comfortable one. He's got a point: this gun does have the sort of feel you get from a pair of cosy slippers, a comfortable friendly kind of gun. That may seem like an odd way to describe a rifle but using some guns is a bit like wrestling an alligator – they're not at all user-friendly. The Ultra is the other end of the scale, being one of the most user-friendly rifles on the market.

The Ultra has a non-removable air reservoir, which is charged in situ via a quick-fill inlet found at the muzzle end of the reservoir. The gun has a 40-shot capacity from a single charge, which is not a lot compared to some other rifles, but from a hunting perspective it is quite sufficient.

Most hunters content themselves with four to six rabbits, or six brace of pigeon. Pest controllers on the other hand, may be taking a hundred-plus pigeons and up to fifty rabbits a time, which would require charging up the Ultra several times during an outing, but this is no great problem.

The slimline reservoir helps to keep the rifle's weight down to just 2.6kg (5.9lb), which is extremely light for a PCP and even lighter than a lot of the spring-powered weapons.

Most PCPs are accurate, but you would have thought the shortness of the Ultra's barrel would not have been able to achieve the same kind of accuracy as a longer barrelled PCP. Yet the Ultra is one of the most accurate rifles I have ever fired. It has been superbly engineered by craftsmen who know their trade well: chocking, crowning, and rifling the barrel with such precision that it delivers consistent pinpoint results.

The short barrel on the Ultra has to be among the very best made barrels found on any air rifle; it is a barrel to be trusted. This barrel is apparently the same one used on the award-winning, top of the range BSA Super Ten, arguably one of the best PCPs ever made, but more about that later.

How to Load and Cock
the Ultra Multi-Shot
Apply the safety catch found on the right-hand side of the gun above the trigger, to the safe position indicated by a white letter S.

With the thumb, disengage the magazine retainer by pushing it forward. The magazine retainer is located on the left-hand side of the rifle just below the point where the barrel enters the breech-block.

Push down with the thumb on the rifle's pellet probe release catch found to the rear of the breech-block on the right-hand side just above the safety catch. The pellet probe will now spring backwards.

Tilt the rifle slightly to the right and insert the fully loaded magazine into the left-hand side of the block, with the probe side of the magazine entering first. When the magazine is seated engage the magazine retainer by pushing it backwards.

Push the pellet probe forward with the right thumb, which delivers the pellet to the barrel. The gun is now loaded but not yet cocked; in other words a pellet is located in the breech ready for discharge but the trigger is not set.

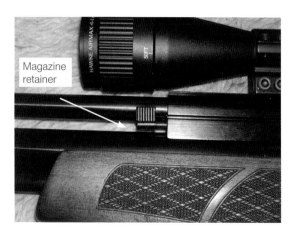

The magazine retainer.

Cock the rifle only when you are ready to shoot. To do this, depress the knob located underneath the air reservoir till you hear a gentle click, which is the trigger engaging. Once the safety catch is removed the gun is ready to fire.

The BSA XL Tactical

The Lightning XL Tactical .22
I would call this rifle the all-weather hunter or the professional pest controller, as it's a real pest controller's weapon. It has everything that the professional looks for in a rifle, being simple, durable and phenomenally reliable.

It is a spring-powered weapon, achieving a power output of 11½ft per lb, making it a very powerful weapon with quite a savage recoil that has to be managed by good technique in the rifle-handling department. It is as tough as granite, you can drop it, knock it, or treat it with contempt and it will take it manfully, not sustaining any damage that would compromise its working ability in any way.

If you want a pure workhorse that can be used anywhere in any weather then you won't go far wrong with this gun. The stock is made from a shock-resistant polymer, which can absorb a considerably heavy blow without sustaining any damage. The stock is also weather resistant, nothing being able to adversely affect it: cold, rain, snow, summer, heat – it is impervious to them all and has a rather unique feature in that the stock is always warm to the touch even when the temperature tips below zero. This, as you can imagine, is a useful feature when hunting in the depths of winter. The stock is not just warm in cold weather, it has a roughened surface to provide grip no matter how slippery the conditions become, and the matt black colouring of the stock means that it is ideal when you want to work in camouflage. A lot of stocks are so shiny you can see the sun glinting of them from half a mile away; such shiny woodwork is visible even when you are in deep cover.

No military sniper would ever consider it worthwhile going out with a gun that was not as well camouflaged as he was. Some airgun hunters recognize that it is a bit silly decking yourself out from head to toe in camouflage and using a gun that is bright and reflective; to deal with the problem they get their guns painted in a camouflage pattern by a specialist. However, the XL Tactical is already halfway there because the dull finish to the stock does not shine or reflect light; so all that needs doing is to have the metalwork dulled down in a similar fashion by having a matt

The super-practical BSA XL Tactical.

paint job, resulting in a gun that will work flawlessly in a camouflage environment.

The stock's shape was designed by computer but that is not to say that the imagination of man played no part. A very skilled stock designer by the name of John Sykes came up with the concept, while a computer did all the mathematical analysis, giving the stock a very precise, balanced finish.

The cheekpiece is raised and curved away from the cheek so that it creates a smooth stock weld, and keeps the head in an erect position giving superb eye alignment with the scope. The pistol grip is also very well shaped, providing good contact with the firing hand that brings the trigger finger into a well-balanced position on the trigger blade. This is achieved by a swelling in the area of the stock where the palm of the firing hand is located, and a groove along the back of the pistol grip designed to receive the thumb. (On a stock without a palm-swell the trigger finger tends to go too far through the trigger, giving a sideways rather than a rearwards pull.) These two innovative features draw the hand to the correct position.

The excellent stock on the Lightning XL Tactical is also hollow. This helps to make the gun nice and light, weighing in at just 3kg (6.6lb), but strangely it feels even lighter than that, perhaps because the weight is so well distributed.

Some PCPs are very heavy lumps indeed and when you have carried them around constantly for three or four hours over rough terrain, around the stage when your arms feel like they are going to drop off at the shoulder, you will be wishing they weren't so darned heavy! But you would have no such thoughts about the XL because it is such a doddle to carry around. Don't, however, get the impression that the XL Tactical is so light that it sways around in the merest breeze while you are trying to take aim; on the contrary, it falls happily into that rare category of not being too heavy or too light – just right in fact.

The XL Tactical like all BSAs from the very bottom to the very top of their range is fitted with a high-quality barrel. The XL Tactical has a carbine-length barrel sleeved by a slimline silencer that does help to reduce the gun's muzzle blast; a silencer however can do nothing to quieten the noise of the action, so to get the very best from this gun I would have it tuned. (The same applies to all spring-powered weapons.) The silencer also works as a cocking aid, helping to reduce the mechanical effort required to cock the weapon.

On top of the compression cylinder, the XL Tactical is very sensibly fitted with a scope rail with a rubber cushion underneath, it absorbs a fair degree of the shock being transmitted to the scope by the recoil of the action. This is one of the rifle's most valuable innovations, and is something to be prized because there are so many spring-guns on the market that offer no dampening system whatsoever below the scope; as a consequence the scope can often lose its zero or, worse, be damaged by the recoil.

The safety catch, located just above the trigger on the right-hand side, disengages smoothly. If you place your thumb on top of the safety catch and control its forward movement as it disengages, rather than allowing it to travel freely, it can be disengaged silently, not making the slightest sound. This makes it the quietest safety catch I have ever come across; even the far more expensive rifles that I have do not have a safety catch as quiet as the XL Tactical. A silent safety catch is a remarkably useful feature: the slightest click and your bunny or pigeon could take fright and disappear.

The blueing of the compression cylinder and barrel will, in common with most air rifles, rust rapidly if not kept well oiled. The finish on the silencer will chip off if it receives a heavy blow, but the same can be said of many silencers and, like other silencers, it does ring a bit if you happen to catch it on a tree branch or something similar.

The XL Tactical .177

The .177 version of the XL Tactical is a very hard-hitting weapon. In fact, when I tested it I was quite surprised by how much power it packed. (I had to check it to make sure I hadn't been sent an FAC version by mistake.) It seemed so much more than 11½ft per lb – literally smashing into whatever I fired at.

The .177 is a pure killing machine, well able to dispatch the full range of quarry that an airgun hunter can pursue. The only problem is the degree of over-penetration: the pellet does not dissipate as much of its energy on impact as I would like. The .177 XL Tactical is, however, a very accurate gun as long as you handle it correctly. You will hit more than you would with the .22, but will do less damage.

At present, the Lightning XL Tactical is considered by many experts to be the best spring-powered hunting rifle on the market, and I agree with their assessment.

The XL Tactical .25

When working at close range, .177 and .22 over-penetrate, going in one side of the quarry and out the other like an express train. .25 will not. It will stay inside the animal you shoot at.

Weighing about 19 grains, the .25 pellet is a monster of a thing, and it is the size of the .25 pellet that causes it to dissipate nearly all of its energy at the point of impact, causing a massive amount of shock that is instantly fatal. The XL Tactical in .25 is an absolute destroyer of a weapon. When it hits quarry it literally lifts the bird or rabbit off its feet. With such power, the XL Tactical allows you to take chest shots at birds or rabbits and, as long as you go for the heart and lungs, the effect will be instantaneous death. The dissipation of energy upon impact, a major feature of the .25 pellet, is due to its high level of drag which makes it a low velocity projectile.

This is without doubt one of the cleanest killing guns on the market. The pellet fired does so much damage that injuries just don't occur (except as a result of appalling marksmanship). Despite what many shooters say about the .25, this weapon will shoot effectively out to 30yd (27m).

The correct pellet for the XL Tactical is the Milbro Rhino; this is the one that best fits the barrel. I really like the .25 XL Tactical, and I am seriously thinking of putting down my .22 and using this .25 instead. I know the .22 gives me a flatter trjectory, but there is nothing that can match tthe .25's knock-down power, and that's what I like. However, I wouldn't suggest that a complete beginner takes up using this weapon as it requires a high degree of skill to control the substantial recoil, and the steep trajectory takes time to master.

For pest controllers working at close range inside agricultural or industrial buildings, this is the perfect weapon. You can take chest shots, which is safer as the target is a lot larger than the head, and you will get no over-penetration whatsoever. This gun is also excellent for close-range rat work: there is no need to aim for the rat's tiny little head; just go straight for the chest and the rat will be bowled over as though it had been hit with a brick.

How to Load and Cock the XL Tactical

Ensure that the safety catch on the right-hand side of the gun, just above the trigger, is engaged. The safe position is indicated by an S letter engraved into the side of the compression cylinder.

With your fingers clear of the trigger area, take a firm hold of the pistol grip area, resting the butt plate on your thigh. Then take a hold of the end of the barrel with your other hand and pull down. You will feel some resistance in the downward pull as the spring in this weapon is very powerful. Once you hear the trigger engage, stop pulling on the barrel.

Take a pellet and insert it into the breech end of the barrel nose, pushing the pellet down until the skirt of the pellet is flush with

Cocking the XL Tactical: compressing the spring using the barrel as a lever to do this.

the end of the barrel. If the skirt of the pellet protrudes from the barrel it will be sheared off when the barrel is closed, which obviously has a seriously negative impact upon the pellet's performance.

Return the barrel to the closed position, making sure you hear it click securely into place. This tells you that the barrel latch has locked into place below the barrel-stop pin.

The weapon is now ready to fire once the safety catch has been moved forward to the F position.

If you were to neglect setting the safety catch and had the rifle cocked waiting to receive a

Closing the barrel.

pellet, and you accidentally depressed the trigger, the barrel would slam violently shut, the stock would probably shatter, and the barrel would be damaged, not to mention the fact that you could sustain a serious injury. So always make sure that the safety goes on, even if there is quarry in front of you and you are in a hurry to get the next pellet loaded. Those who neglect the safety aspect of the sport will sooner or later end up injuring themselves or someone else.

A carbine like the XL Tactical should never be fired without the silencer in place. Frankly, it is dangerous. Never remove it.

The BSA Super Ten Mk3 Bull Barrel

I would call this rifle the ultimate. It is without doubt the ultimate hunting machine and it is not just me who concludes this. The air rifle industry were so impressed by this gun's design and performance that they awarded it the coveted Airgun of the Year award.

Let's begin with what I have identified as one of a weapon's most important features, the barrel. The Super Ten is equipped with a match-standard barrel, which means this barrel is of the same high specification as those used on competition target rifles; thus, very

particular attention has been paid to the barrel's engineering. The gunsmiths have worked to a high spec, creating a barrel that has the capacity for tremendous accuracy. Even a mediocre shot can achieve and experience some tremendous results with this rifle, and, in the hands of the more competent, groups of a sub-inch nature are achieved without too much effort time and again. The Super Ten has to be without doubt one of the most accurate hunting air weapons ever produced.

There are two versions of Super Ten: one with a standard barrel and one with a shrouded barrel; the latter comes as a bull barrel (short carbine length), or rifle (standard barrel length).

Why shroud a barrel? Many will say it's for nothing more than looks, and there is no doubt that a shrouded barrel looks jolly impressive. But there is a lot more to it than that. The shroud provides protection for the barrel. Barrels are made from steel and need constant oiling to prevent rust. With a shrouded barrel, the barrel is encased in a tube so it is protected from the elements as well as any knocks and scrapes that come its way. The shroud is made from anodized aluminium so it does not rust.

The high-class BSA Super Ten bull barrel carbine.

The shroud on the Super Ten also forms the housing for a very sophisticated silencer, with spring-mounted baffles that are extremely effective at combating the weapon's muzzle blast, making for one of the quietest on the market. Where many rifles speak, the Super Ten merely whispers as the pellet hurries on its way. Though a shrouded barrel is a little bit more expensive than the non-shrouded version it's money worth paying, as from the hunter's perspective the shroud provides a level of barrel protection that warrants the extra cost.

So which of the shrouded versions of the Super Ten – carbine or rifle length – is the one for you? Don't base your decision on looks but upon the kind of shooting you are going to do. If you're going to be more concerned with pest control, with quarry such as feral pigeons and rats, working in and around farm buildings or industrial premises, then go for the carbine version. It is very short, measuring just 33½in (85cm), and therefore very manoeuvrable in the confined spaces that such shooting presents. However, if long-range rabbit shooting is your game then go for the shrouded barrel with a rifle length.

The rifle's barrel measures 37½in (95cm); that extra 4in (10cm) means that the pellet will receive more rotation as it moves down the barrel which will give it more stability in flight. A definite advantage when working at long-range, as that should help to preserve the pellet's accuracy. The only slight concern I have about the shrouded barrels is the fact that the removal of the barrel requires the services of a gunsmith, whereas the barrel on the standard non-shrouded version can be easily removed by loosening two allen-headed bolts.

The air supply for the Super Ten is contained not in an integral air cylinder, but in what is termed a buddy bottle: a small air vessel that has to be removed from the rifle for refilling. The operation of removing and refilling the buddy bottle may take a bit longer to perform than is the case with a weapon that has an integral air cylinder. However, the buddy bottle offers a larger cubic capacity, so you get more shots from a single charge of a buddy bottle than you do from a single charge of an integral air cylinder. The Super Ten (rifle version), for example, offers around 230 shots per charge in .22 calibre, whereas the BSA Hornet (rifle version) – a gun with an integral air cylinder in the same calibre – offers around 170 shots per charge which, it has to be said, is rather a lot for a weapon with an integral air cylinder. Many of the other manufacturers can only manage to get 70 to 90 shots out of a gun with an integral air cylinder. So quick-fill systems save time but you get fewer shots per charge.

The other thing about a buddy bottle that I ought to mention is that you can carry a spare in your game bag. With an integral air cylinder, you need to have a charging system on hand to refill. A charging system is a lot more cumbersome to carry into the field than a back-up buddy bottle.

The Super Ten is a bolt-action weapon. The bolt, located on the right-hand side of the block, is a very chunky and robust piece of metalwork, meaning that it is easy to handle and does not flinch in the face of rough treatment. The ease with which the bolt slides means that even a child (if correctly supervised) can operate it, though the rifle would have to be supported in some way as it's rather heavy.

It has a crisp, very rapid action, making it one of the quickest weapons to load that I have ever used. A rapid loading system is sometimes very useful when an animal is injured, for example, and a second shot is required as quickly as possible. A rapid loading mechanism can also be very useful if feral pigeons are the target quarry. You can often be presented with a large numbers of ferals in a roof space that will be unnerved at the first shot; you then have a limited amount of time – usually seconds rather than minutes – to bring down a few further pigeons before they make their escape. The Super Ten is well suited to such work. The rapid pellet delivery in combination with the correct scope will give very speedy target acquisition and despatch. I do not know of a gun that can deliver a pellet to the barrel quicker than the Super Ten. For this reason, I rate the carbine length Super Ten as the ultimate feral pigeon gun.

Weight is the weapon's only real downside, which, depending on the version, varies from 7.7lb (3.5kg) to 9lb (4kg), and that's quite a lot for a rifle. The weight was bound to be a little on the heavy side owing to all the features it possesses. One positive effect of the weight is stability. If you rest this rifle on a bale of straw, for example, to line up and take your shot, it will not be buffeted by the wind. Some rifles are so light that the slightest puff of wind or the tiniest movement in the shooter's body can move them off line. The Super Ten is therefore a heavy lump to carry around (this of course could be obviated by fitting a sling), but when placed in a supported firing position it is as solid as the good old rock of Gibraltar.

The Super Ten is fed by the BSA patented ten-shot magazine, which they use in all their rifles (this is as near perfect as possible for a hunting weapon).

The safety catch on the Super Ten, located to the right-hand side of the stock just beneath the bolt, is recessed into the woodwork so that no part of the catch protrudes from the side of the rifle. Many guns, some very expensive ones included, have the safety catch protruding in the most vulnerable manner which makes it very susceptible to damage. I have known safety catches of this design to be knocked clean off the rifle the first time they were used in the field.

Recessing the safety catch like this also helps to guard against an accidental disengagement of the safety catch. It has to be said that the designers of this rifle, who include the somewhat legendary gunsmith John Bowkett, did not go for gimmicks, but looked at what the hunter really needs and made a rifle to meet all those needs with bells on.

Now we are going to move on to the most amazing trigger you will find on a hunting air rifle. In my opinion it's the best hunting trigger on the market. It is a beautifully smooth trigger, with the facility to adjust the load so that it can be made even lighter if required. The trigger also has features that allow the height and angle of the trigger blade to be adjusted, so that the trigger can be bespoke to match the exact requirements of your trigger finger. Some have short fingers, others long, some thin, and some fat: different fingers require different positions on the trigger blade.

On most triggers you adopt a position that is as close as possible to perfect, but with the Super Ten you can set the blade so that the perfect position can be taken up. This is a phenomenal advantage that actually turns a mediocre shot into a good one. The reason for this is quite simple: the less effort required to pull the trigger, the less disturbance the gun will experience; therefore, the more accurate the shot. Also, by setting the blade of the trigger to respond to the individual features of your trigger finger, you are ensuring a trigger pull that has only a rearward movement with no sideways disturbance. Target shooters have a trigger like this because it makes for greater accuracy.

Not only is the trigger fully adjustable, the butt plate is as well. By releasing a screw, the plate can be moved so that it marries up to the peculiarities of your anatomy, making it extremely comfortable to shoulder but, more importantly, making you and the gun more streamlined and a more stable unit. The coarser the fit of the rifle to the shoulder, the less accuracy you can achieve, which is why target rifles have an adjustable butt plate. So again, the adjustability of the Super Ten's butt plate will make you a better shot.

Before moving on to the Super Ten's all important killing ability, let's just stop to take a look at the scope rail and stock. The scope rail is in one continuous piece, going straight over the top of the magazine. Many PCPs have a two-piece scope rail, positioned at the front and rear of the magazine.

The one-piece rail is a much better design as it allows much more room for the adjustment of the scope mounts; the two-piece scope rail offers very limited room for adjustment and, sometimes, a special set of mounts has to be used to deal with this lack of adjustability. The one-piece rail is infinitely preferable and a lot easier to use. If I had the choice between two rifles of equal ability that differed in only one respect – one had a two-piece scope rail and the other had a one-piece – I would choose the rifle with the one-piece scope rail every time.

The stock on the Super Ten is a very tough piece of wood that can take the knocks. My rifles take a real beating, getting smashed up against all kinds of abrasive objects that can ruin a stock in weeks. But the Super Ten's stock was up to the rough treatment, so don't get the idea that because this gun is such a high-tech weapon it is somewhat delicate. Far from it. This is a robust piece of quality engineering, able to take whatever the environment has to throw at it. Despite being exposed to the appalling Scottish weather over an extended period of time, I haven't seen one single speck of rust appear on the Super Ten, which is quite a remarkable feat for the environment in which I live – the sea is only a few miles away and the air is laden heavily with salt, which manages to make very quick inroads on even the best protected metal.

The stock also provides a most excellent gripping surface, even in slippery conditions; the chequering around the pistol grip and the forestock is more deeply cut than normally seen and has a more pronounced effect, which offers a high level of resistance, thus a firmer grip. The cheekpiece on the stock is quite high and curves smoothly away from the cheek, so as to give the head an erect position with excellent eye alignment to the scope.

Now let us get on with the nitty gritty side of things: the Super Ten's killing ability. It is of course a full powered weapon with 11½ft per lb of energy in every shot, but as I have already stated, and will continue to do so, this is only part of the story. What we need to know as hunters is, what does that energy do when it strikes the quarry?

The chequering on the Super Ten is some of the finest you will see.

On my range, the backstop is a piece of corrugated tin with a sloping bank of soil in front of it. At the top, the slope is about 10–15cm (4–6in) deep, which should be sufficient to exhaust any pellet of all its energy after passing through the target; but not so with a pellet fired from the Super Ten. A pellet fired from the Super Ten goes straight though that 10–15cm (4–6in) of soil and strikes the tin at the back, making a plinking sound as it does so. I removed the soil to see what kind of impact the pellet was having on the tin and, to my surprise I discovered that it still had sufficient energy to make a reasonable dent in the tin.

I even tried the Super Ten on 10cm (4in) of compacted sand, which I rammed into an old tin can. The pellet ripped through the front of the can, which was no surprise, but then it drilled straight through the sand in an almost straight line and nearly exited the back. This is a phenomenal level of penetration – a bit too

The raised curved cheekpiece on the Super Ten makes for a very comfortable stock weld.

much for close-range pest control – but absolutely spot on for long-range rabbit shooting.

As a rule, 30yd (27m) is the maximum range at which I will shoot with an air rifle. The Super Ten, is the only rifle with which I would consider shooting from a greater range because of its accuracy and penetration. A pellet fired from this gun at a rabbit's head, even at distances of 35yd (32m), will smash through the skull as if it were an eggshell, going straight through the brain and causing catastrophic damage; then, maintaining its line, it will more than likely exit the other side of the rabbit's head and bury itself in the ground. This gun is a very serious killing machine.

The Super Ten is fitted with a regulator, a feature that you normally get in customized rifles. It ensures that every single shot has exactly the same amount of air behind it; this is achieved by regulating the discharge from the air cylinder. When a regulator is not present, tiny variations will occur in the amount of air released from the air cylinder from shot to shot, and so the trajectory of each shot is marginally different. On a rifle fitted with a regulator, such variations do not occur so the trajectory from shot to shot is more uniform, which is another reason why the Super Ten is so accurate. But such sophisticated engineering does not come cheap. A Super Ten will

cost in the region of £650 to £700 (at the time of writing), so it may be something to aspire to rather than to begin with. For the shooter who wants everything, however, this gun fits the bill.

How to Load and Cock the BSA Super Ten

First, ensure that the safety catch located on the right-hand side of the rifle, below the bolt, is engaged. This is done by sliding the catch towards the rear of the rifle so that it covers the red dot that you will see in the recess where the safety catch is located.

Grasp the bolt handle and pull it back; when it reaches the end of its rearward travel push it down into rear holding position.

Place a loaded magazine into the breech-block; it enters from the left-hand side of the rifle. The side of the magazine that has a probe is the side that enters the breech-block first.

Grasp the bolt handle and slide it out of the rear holding position; push it forwards and down into the forward holding position. Make sure the bolt handle goes into the forward holding position or you will have an escape of air when you fire the weapon.

The weapon is now ready to fire. All that is required is to remove the safety catch before you take your shot.

CHAPTER THREE

Scopes

Scopes can be very confusing pieces of equipment for the uninitiated so, before I launch into this chapter, there follows here a guide to the terms that describe the various features found on a modern hunting scope.

Body Tube
If you look at a scope, you will see there is a lens either end, and where the lenses are located the housing raises up to incorporate them. Between these two raised areas, is a parallel section referred to as the body tube which measures 1in (25mm) in circumference.

Lens
There is a lens at either end of the scope, one at the rear that you look through (the ocular lens) and one at the front (the obective lens) through which the light enters the scope. The front lens is the objective lens. The size of this lens is measured in millimetres and is the second figure after the × on a scope designation. So, in 3–9×40, 40 is the size of the lens (40mm).

Eyebell (Eye Box)
The part of the scope that houses the ocular lens and the focusing system.

Power Change Ring (Magnification Ring)
Just in front of the eyebell you will see a movable ring marked up with figures, the most common set of figures being from three to nine. These figures represent the level of

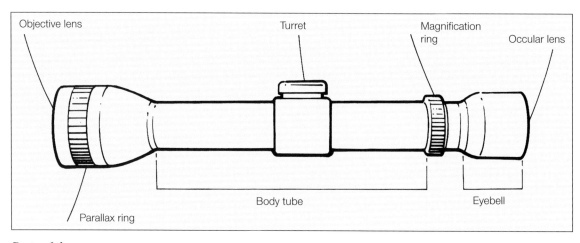

Parts of the scope.

magnification (three is therefore three times magnification). Magnification is a measure of how much closer an object appears when viewed through a scope.

A scope set on three times magnification will make distant objects appear to be three times closer than they actually are. A scope marked from three to nine means that the magnification can be increased from three to nine in increments of one. Just to the rear of the power change ring on the eyebell you will find a marking of some kind, usually a very obvious white dot; one of the figures on the ring lined up with the dot indicates the level of magnification the scope will be operating under.

The symbol × is used to indicate magnification, e.g. 6× means six times magnification; 3–9× means that there is an adjustable magnification system that can vary from three times magnification to nine times. So if a scope has a designation of 3–9×40, that would mean it had a variable magnification capacity from three to nine times magnification and an objective lens measuring 40mm.

Saddle
In the centre of the body tube you will see a bulging section with a turret on top and another sticking out of its side. The bulging bit is known as the saddle.

Reticle
If you look through the scope you will see an aiming grid, usually two lines as thin as a hair in the shape of a cross, known as the cross-hairs. But the aiming grid could have another pattern, a dot for example, or something called a 30/30 (we shall look at all the different patterns later, for now all you need to know is that there is more than one pattern). Whatever aiming grid is inside a scope, whether it is the cross-hairs or something else, it is known as the reticle.

Turrets
Sitting on top of the saddle is the elevation turret, found under a removable protective

covering known as a turret cap. To the right, housed within the saddle, you will find the windage turret, again located under a cap. The turrets are rotating adjusters that can move the position of the reticle.

If we take as our example the most commonly known reticle, the cross-hairs, the elevation turret moves the position of the horizontal cross-hair and the windage turret moves the position of the vertical cross-hair. The turrets adjust the reticle in increments known as MOA. MOA stands for 'minutes of angle'; it's a measuring system that equates to 1in of movement at 100yd.

One click of the turret (one turn – the term click is used because it is the sound that the turret makes as it rotates) will move the cross-hair one MOA in the desired direction, meaning that the projectile will strike the target 1in away from the previous shot at 100yd distance.

If we made this adjustment to the elevation turret, we would move the strike point of the projectile 1in higher or lower, depending on which way we rotated it. The same adjustment to the windage turret will move the strike point of the projectile 1in left or right. The further away the target is, the greater the level of adjustment in the strike point from one MOA of movement. Thus, one MOA at 200yd would effect a movement on the projectile's striking point of 2in, and at 500yd a movement of 5in.

The converse is also true: the closer the target, the less the level of adjustment. A target at 50yd would therefore reduce the adjustment of just ½in. Just to complicate matters, the type of scope you will be using on your air rifle will have a turret adjustment scale of ¼in MOA at 100yd. One click on the turret will equate to a movement in the projectile's strike point on the target of ¼in from the previous shot at a distance of 100yd. Air rifles do not operate at such ranges; an air rifle should be used at 30–35yd, so we need to use a bit of brainpower to calculate what the adjustment will be for a ¼in MOA (one click of the turret) at such short distances.

To find the exact level of adjustment for 30yd, we need to turn ¼in into 10/40 of an inch, so that ¼in MOA equates to 10/40 of an inch at 100yd.

If we now calculate the level of adjustment for 10yd we get 1/40 of an inch. We then simply multiply this by three, and have the level of adjustment at 30yd. 3/40 of an inch tells us that a turret with an adjustment scale of ¼in MOA at 100yd has an adjustment level on the strike point of the pellet of 3/40 of an inch at 30yd. Each click of the turret then moves the strike point of the pellet 3/40 of an inch in the desired direction. If we divide the top figure of 3/40 by the bottom, we'll find the number of clicks required to move the strike point of the pellet by 1in at 30yd, which gives us 13.3. So, 13.3 clicks of the turret at 30yd moves the strike point of the pellet by 1in. Only it will have to be 14 clicks because the turrets do not move by fewer degrees than one.

Parallax Setting
This is the range at which the scope is set up to function. Most good air rifle scopes offer an adjustable parallax setting, which enables the user to select one of a number of ranges. Most of the Hawke scopes start around 30ft (9m) and go up to 25yd (23m), then 50yd (45m). There are further settings beyond this, but they are irrelevant as far as the airgun user is concerned.

The parallax setting can be used as quite an accurate range-finding device. Say, for example, that you have the parallax ring set at 15yd (13m), and you shoulder the rifle and observe the target through the scope; if it presents a crystal clear image then you know that your target is around the 15yd (13m) mark. But if the image is blurred, you know that it must be closer or further than 15yd (13m). (You need to develop good judgement of range to know which of these categories the target falls into.) If, with this example, you judge that the target is further away than 15yd (13m) and you think it is around the 20yd (18m) mark, you would turn the parallax ring to a point short of the 25yd (23m) mark on the ring. (Practice on the range will soon help you to figure out where 20yd (18m) is located on the ring, and you could even mark it up if you wish by applying a small dot of white enamel paint with a 000 size brush.) If your estimate was correct, your target should now present a crystal clear image; if you were incorrect and the image is still blurred, make a further adjustment.

I find that with very high magnification, say 24×, the parallax setting provides a very accurate indicator of range, and is my preferred option for range-finding with long-range shots.

Eye Relief
This is the farthest distance your eye should be from the ocular lens. This distance can vary, the average being around 82mm. But there are scopes with an eye relief as low as 76mm, and others that can be as far away as 89mm. A long eye relief is of particular importance for those shooters who wear glasses.

Field of View (FOV)
This tells you how wide the circle of view is at a distance of 100yd (91m). So let us say that the field of view is 8yd (7.1m). That means that what you see through the scope is an area 8yd (7.1m) in circumference. This is of course irrelevant for the airgun user, so simply halve the figure (I would ignore the .1) which gives us 4yd (3.5m) at 50yd (45m). Halve the figure again, bringing it to 1½yd (1.75m) at 25yd (23m). You now have a fairly accurate indication of what the field of view will be.

A scope with an adjustable magnification facility will have a variable field of view, depending on what magnification is used. The higher the magnification, the smaller the field of view. A scope with a specification of 3–10×44 will offer a field of view that is 13.6–4.26m (at 110yd/100m), the field of view dramatically decreasing as the magnification goes up. For the airgun user, this would give a field of view of approximately 3.4m–105cm (at 25yd/23m).

Lens Coating

Because glass reflects some of the light passing through it, a scope constructed without an anti-reflective coating on the lens surfaces would deliver a very poor darkened image. In order to reduce reflection, and thus improve the quality of the image, the lenses of good scopes are vacuum coated with layers of magnesium fluoride, dramatically increasing the level of light transmission through the scope.

There are various classes of lens coating. These are listed below, beginning with the lowest quality lens covering (judged on degree of light transmission and clarity of image):

- Coated.
  Only some of the lenses have received an anti-reflective coating. This produces a fairly reasonable image at a modest cost.

- Fully coated.
  All the air to glass surfaces have been coated, bringing about a brighter image.

- Multi-coated.
  The manufacturer has applied multiple coatings of anti-reflective material to most of the lenses.

- Fully Multi-Coated.
  This is the most expensive and effective form of lens coating offering optimum light transmission. As such it is top of the tree.

There are some special lenses that have a tint to deal with extremely bright light, but since I live in Scotland and not California I do not really need such a lens. I use the Hawke range of scopes, which are fully multi-coated.

Aim Point

A point on the reticle that is used to aim the rifle. This could be the centre of the crosshairs, a dot, or a bar. It will not always be in the centre of the reticle pattern.

WHY USE A TELESCOPIC SIGHTING DEVICE?

Years ago most shooters, including me, hunted with nothing more than open sights and achieved quite acceptable results. Today however, hardly anybody with a bit of knowledge about the sport would consider entering the field without a telescopic sight fitted to their rifle. Why is this? To explain, we first need to know a little about how sights work.

How Sights Work

The purpose of a sighting system is to place the line of sight and the elevation of the barrel in a reciprocal relationship that enables the gun's trajectory and the line of sight to intersect at the point at which you desire to strike the target. That's a bit of a mouthful! Basically, it means getting the gun barrel to point at the same thing you are looking at.

If a gun was fired while the barrel was in a horizontal position, the pellet would be

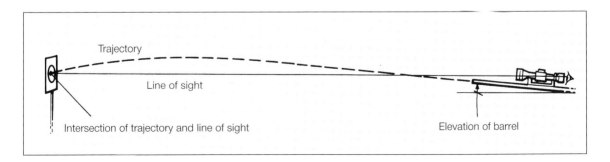

How sights work.

brought down by the forces of gravity long before it reached the desired target. When the correct angle of elevation is chosen, the pellet is able to trace an arc that will bring it on to the required target.

The telescopic sight enables you to select the correct angle of elevation with a far greater degree of precision than could be achieved with open sights. It is not just magnification that makes the telescopic sight superior: it also offers more aim points and infinitely more adjustments.

The telescopic sight is the most humane of sighting systems. One of the main reasons for this is that it magnifies the target, making it much easier to precisely position the aim point on the target's kill zone than it would be with open sights. This makes the telescopic sight an essential piece of equipment.

I used to do a lot of beating in the fields and woods of Cambridgeshire for some very prestigious shoots. During that time, I saw many pheasants injured: some could not continue to fly and fell to the ground to be retrieved by eager dogs, but others struggled on their way, probably to die later of blood loss or some form of sepsis. The shotgun is a fairly brutal weapon that targets the entire body mass. On the shoots I was involved with, using a shotgun led to at least 20 per cent of the birds receiving injuries rather than being killed.

The telescopic sight on the other hand, allows for a much more precise placement of the projectile, allowing the shooter to position it right in the brain of the target. The precision of the telescopic sight means much less injured quarry. I would estimate that the quarry I happen to injure in the course of a year's shooting would be 3 to 4 per cent.

ZEROING, RANGE-FINDING AND WINDAGE

Zeroing

Zeroing is the act of calibrating the eye, scope, and barrel elevation so that they all align with one another in order to deliver the pellet to the required point on the target.

You zero a rifle into a desired range using the centre cross of the reticle. Let us say that the desired range was 25yd (23m). Once zeroed, the rifle will deliver an accurate placement of shots at the 25yd (23m) range. You would miss if you used the centre cross on a target closer or further away than 25yd (23m). Zeroing is range-specific: when the range changes, the zero must also change.

Depending on the type of reticle you are using, there are several different methods of doing this; we shall look at the different reticles and their usage later. You first need to select the range at which you wish to zero your rifle, the table opposite should help you.

Zeroing should take place on a day when there is no perceptible wind speed.

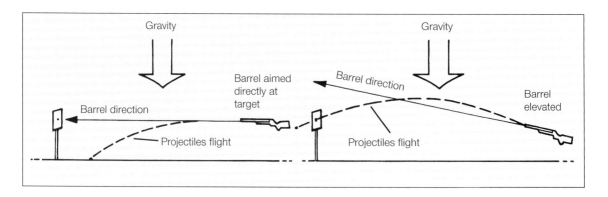

The effect of gravity upon trajectory.

Range settings for different quarry

Quarry	Type of scope	Zero range	Magnification
Rat	Low magnification, wide field of view	10/15yd (9/13m)	×1.5 or ×2
Pigeon, feral	Low magnification, wide field of view	10/15yd (9/13m)	×1.5 or ×2
Pigeon, Wood	High magnification	30yd (27m)	×18 or ×20
Rabbit, lamping	Wide objective lens	25yd (23m)	×06 or ×14
Rabbit, daytime	High magnification	30yd (27m)	×18 or ×20
Various quarry	General-purpose scope	25yd (23m)	×9 or ×12

The Zeroing Process

1. Set up a target on your range at the distance you wish the rifle to be zeroed to. Make sure the target is fairly large; the scope could be well away from the desired zero and could be 15, 20 or even 30cm (6, 8, 12in) off, so you won't even hit a small A4 target.

   I use an old feed bag, such as used for dog or chicken feed. I cut it open so that it makes a 1 × 1m (3 × 3ft) sheet, which I pin to my target holder. I then place a piece of coloured tape at the centre of the sheet to act as my desired target area.

2. Remove the turret caps from the elevation and windage turrets and place them in a safe place.

3. Set your parallax to the desired distance and select your magnification.

4. Load your weapon and take up a supported firing position: stand, kneel, or lie down, whatever you like but you must have the rifle well supported. This is best achieved by using a tripod or by resting the rifle on an object of some kind.

5. Use the centre of the cross-hairs and line them up with the mark on the target. Take your time and remember to use good technique. When you are ready, fire the first shot. Don't concern yourself at this stage with where the shot has landed, instead reload and fire again, fire a third shot – each shot lining up the centre of the cross-hairs with the mark on the target.

6. Go to the target and see where the three shots have landed, taking with you a ruler and a pen. Measure how far to the left or right you are from the mark in millimetres, and write the figure next to your shots; then measure how far above or below the mark your shots fell, and write this down also. Measure from the central point, between the three shots (*see* diagram overleaf). Before returning to the rifle to make adjustments, you must first work out how much adjustment is required. This is easily done with the help of the table below.

Turret adjustments

	5yd	10yd	15yd	20yd	25yd	30yd
Four clicks of the turret equals	1.2mm	2.4mm	3.6mm	4.8mm	6mm	7.2mm

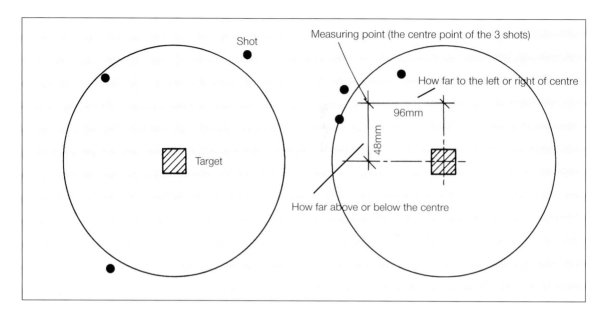

This kind of pattern where shots fall randomly around the target shows inconsistent technique. Further adjustment to the turrets is hopeless at this stage. Keep practising your technique to tighten up the grouping of the shots.

These missed shots are more tightly grouped and so adjustments to the turrets are feasible. (Even if these shots were 6–10in or even 12in from the target, adjustments are still feasible. It is a grouping you are after. Proximity to the target is irrelevant.)

If you take as an example the diagram above, the mark was missed by 96mm to the left and by 48mm below. Therefore, we need to make an adjustment that equates to 96mm on the windage turret moving to the right, and an adjustment on the elevation turret that equates to 48mm moving downwards. To figure out how many clicks are required on each turret, a simple bit of maths is involved.

First, take the four-click adjustment for the range at which you are working; our range is 25yd (23m), so we take the figure 6mm. Next, take the distance you are off the mark, which for the windage is 96mm. Divide 96mm by 6mm (giving us 16). Multiply this by 4 to give you the number of clicks you will be required to apply to the windage turret.

The result is 64 clicks to the right. For the elevation the same principle is applied:

$$\frac{48}{6} = 8 \times 4 = 32 \text{ clicks in the down direction.}$$

7. Return to the rifle and make the adjustments that you have just worked out.
8. Fire three more shots at your mark using the centre of the cross-hairs.
9. Return to your target with a pair of compasses and draw a circle around your mark that equates to your level of marksmanship (*see* diagram opposite). Set your compasses at half the width of the circle that you have chosen, in order to create a circle of the correct width. Alternatively, like me, you can have a set of discs pre-cut in stout cardboard. If all three shots fall within the circle you have chosen then your rifle is zeroed. For hunting purposes you will need to keep practising until you can achieve a grouping of 1½in (3cm), which means all three shots falling within a 1½in (3cm) circle.
10. If some of your shots fall inside and some outside the circle, it may be necessary to make some adjustments (*see* diagram overleaf). If fine adjustments are

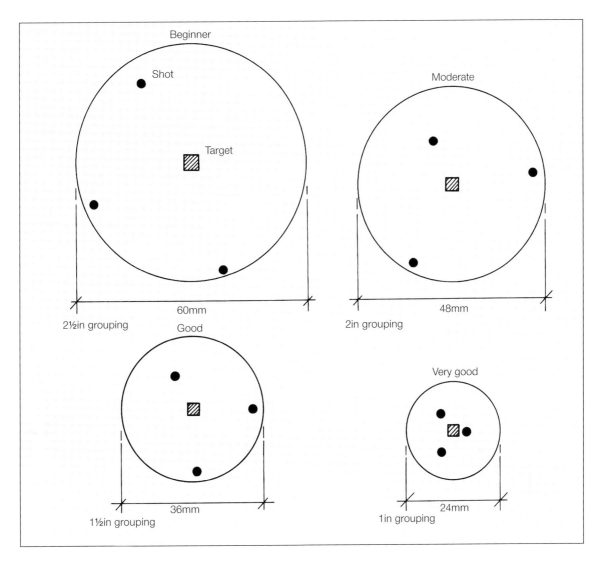

Standard of shooting measured by grouping.

necessary, measure the distance from the missed shots to the outer of the grouping circle. Let us say one missed shot is 2mm out and the other 6mm. Take the middle difference between these two figures, which is 4mm, and apply an adjustment to the turret that would bring about a 4mm movement of the shot's placement. At 25yd (23m), we know that four clicks equals 6mm, so two clicks would equal 3mm. Apply the

two clicks; if you still need to move the shot over apply a third.

Though the rifle is now precisely zeroed, you will need to check it before every hunting trip (by firing two sets of three shots) to ensure that the zero has remained constant.

Range-finding

Range-finding (calculating the distance from you to the target) is integral to bringing about

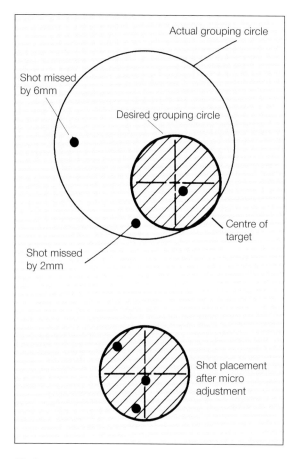

Actual grouping circle

Shot missed
by 6mm

Desired grouping circle

Centre of
target

Shot missed
by 2mm

Shot placement
after micro
adjustment

Tightening a 1½in grouping. A micro-adjustment of 4mm will tighten the grouping.

a successful shot. Get this right and you have a clean kill; get it wrong and you miss by a mile or, worse, you injure your quarry. Range-finding is the first step for taking a shot; if you do not have a range you do not know what parallax setting is required, or what aim point to focus on the target's kill zone, or even what magnification to use.

The curved trajectory of an air weapon means that if you are to hit the target your calculation of the target's range has to be accurate to within 5yd (5m) of its actual distance when using a .177, and to within 2yd/2m for .22. Most people are very poor at estimating distances, but if you practise this skill on a daily basis you will find that you are soon able to accurately calculate distance.

As you are about your daily business, pick out an object ahead of you and estimate its distance, then pace it out. At the beginning you will be astonished how far out you are, but fairly quickly your eye will begin to develop a sense for distance, so getting to within 5yd (5m) of an object's actual distance should be no problem. Until you can do this you should not start hunting. Until you are proficient at it you cannot guarantee a clean kill.

There are all sorts of range-finding devices on the market that can do the job, but to me it seems a shame that so many shooters are abandoning natural skills for electronic devices. There is much talk these days of man's environmental impact on the world, and it is certain that the human eye working in conjunction with the human brain is more environmentally friendly than some electronic laser device that works off batteries. I shall stick to using the human eye, keeping alive the ancient skills used by our forefathers.

There are situations where the eye is challenged and can be deceived. The following list will help you to recognize such situations.

Nature of the Target
An object of regular outline such as a water trough will appear to be closer than an object with an irregular outline, such as a clump of grass.

A partially revealed target such as a rabbit's head sticking out of the undergrowth will appear more distant than it actually is.

A target that contrasts with its background – a rabbit sat out in the snow for example – will appear more distant than it actually is.

Nature of the Ground
Range-finding over smooth surfaces, such as sand or snow, can cause the hunter to underestimate the distance to the target.

When range-finding downhill, the target will seem to be further away than it is; when looking uphill the target will appear closer.

When looking down a row of trees, such as you find at the edge of woodlands, the target will appear to be further away than it is.

When range-finding over ground that has a dip in it, the target will seem more distant than it is in reality.

Light Conditions

Another challenge to the human eye is poor light. Humans have few rods and cones within the eye to see clearly in poor light conditions, unlike the cat, but the more time spent in such conditions the better your abilities become. Like all other aspects of shooting, practice is the keyword.

The more clearly a target can be seen the closer it appears.

When the sun gets behind a target, it will make that target appear to be at a greater distance than it actually is, and it will be very difficult to see. It is therefore best to try to get the sun behind you, which has the effect of making the target appear closer than it is.

In short, range-finding is not nearly as complicated as it sounds, all you need to do is teach your brain what a certain distance looks like and learn to recognize those situations that can trick the eye. The human brain is an amazing thing, far superior to any computer: the amount of information it can process is staggering, so use it – not some range-finding device.

I know that my approach may seem to some a little old-fashioned, but let us not forget that supremely effective hunters took handsome bags of game long before range-finding devices became so widely used, so let's not be so quick to abandon the old ways altogether.

Range-finding with the Parallax Ring

The parallax ring on most good-quality scopes is adjustable and can be precisely set at a given range. Say, for example, you chose to set the parallax at 25yd (23m) then looked through the lenses. A target at 25yd (23m) distance would be in clear focus, but a closer target, say one at 20yd (18m), would be blurred as would a more distant target, 30yd (27m) for example. As you can see, it is quite easy to use the parallax ring of a scope to estimate the distance a target is away from you.

Simply estimate the range to the desired target and set the parallax at that range, if the target is blurred you know that you were incorrect. By adjusting the parallax up or down till the target presents a clear image, you can get an accurate estimate of range. Some shooters say that using a parallax ring to estimate distance is not very accurate, but I have found that the Hawke range of scopes has a very precise parallax ring that is accurate to within several yards. The only slight problem, is that the parallax ring is marked in increments of 50yd, 25yd, and 15yd.

As an airgun shooter, you really need in addition to these markings a 35yd, 30yd, and 20yd marker. This can be accomplished by going to the range with your rifle, a small pot of enamel paint and a very fine artist's brush. Place a target at 35yd (32m) and adjust the parallax ring till the target is in perfect focus, now paint a fine white line on the parallax ring and write beneath it 32/35 to denote the mark for 35yd (32m). Do the same for 30yd (27m) and 20yd (18m). Customizing a scope in this way is how the shooter manages to get the very best out of his equipment.

Some shooters might say that painting markers onto the scope will ruin its looks, but I am of the opinion that a scope is to be used and not looked at.

(NB The higher the mag setting the more accurate the parallax adjuster.)

Windage

Windage is the effect wind has on the flight of the pellet. The wind presents a huge problem for the hunter, simply because the wind by its very nature is so unpredictable. Crosswinds, even very mild ones, have the effect of blowing the pellet off its line by a considerable amount.

At a distance of 35yd (32m), a gentle breeze of just 3mph can blow a .22 pellet anywhere between 20 and 60mm off target; a .177 pellet off its line between 13 and 25mm. The .22 is blown off line by around twice as much as the .177 pellet, simply because it is a bigger object

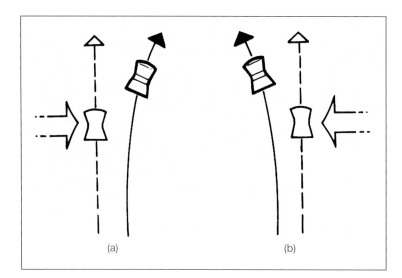

(a) Wind from the left blows pellet to the right. (b) Wind from the right blows pellet to the left.

with a larger surface area, it also travels more slowly than the .177 pellet.

The first thing to note is that if you are going to be shooting in windy conditions on a regular basis, then you are better off being equipped with a .177 weapon. In order for the hunter to hit his desired target, he must compensate for the effect of the wind on his pellet or he will never hit anything. The hunter must be able to read the wind. This begins by determining the wind direction: does it come from the left or right. Winds from the left will blow the pellet to the right, and winds from the right will blow pellets to the left.

Determining wind direction is simplicity itself, all you need to do is tie a light piece of thread, heavy cotton, or a piece of wool to the end of your gun barrel. All that is required, is for you to observe which direction the wind is blowing the thread. I have a small chicken feather attached to the barrel of my rifle and it is very effective indeed. Once you have established the wind direction, you know which way you will have to move the aim point to compensate for the wind.

If the wind was coming from the left, you would move the aim point to the right, shooting into the wind (you always shoot into the wind) so that the pellet will drift onto the target. The skill comes in knowing how far to move the aim point. Move too little and the pellet will still be blown off target, too much and it will fall short. To figure out how much movement is required in the aim point, we need to know the wind speed. This is achieved by reading your environment. The table below will show you what to look for.

Wind speeds of 22–30km/h (12–16mph) are the maximum strength of wind that the airgun hunter can hunt in, and that is only if you are very good marksman. For most, a maximum wind strength of around 18km/h (10mph) would be more appropriate.

Now that we have a rough estimate of the wind speed, we need also to take into account the angle at which the wind is blowing. The angle determines the power of the wind's effect upon the pellet. A wind coming from 90 degrees for example, will exhibit its full power upon the pellet, whereas a wind coming in at 45 degrees will exhibit only half of its power upon the pellet (*see* upper diagram overleaf). A 5km/h (3mph) wind coming in at 90 degrees will be taken at full power, whereas the same 5km/h wind coming in at 45 degrees will exhibit only the power of a 2.5km/h (1½mph) wind.

Now we have all the required information regarding the wind, we need to know how to interpret this to the movement of the aim

Assessing the wind

Description of wind	Wind speed		Environmental signs
	km/h	*(mph)*	
Calm	Less than 1.5	1	Smoke rises vertically and leaves do not stir
Slight air movement	Less than 5	3	Wind can hardly be felt but smoke will begin to drift
Light breeze	5–9	3–5	Wind felt on face and leaves begin to rustle
Gentle breeze	9–15	5–8	Leaves in constant motion
Moderate breeze	15–22	8–12	Small branches move
Fresh breeze	22–30	12–16	Small trees in leaf sway and the tops of tall trees in noticeable motion
Strong breeze	30–37	16–20	Large branches in motion and whistling heard in wires
Near gale	37–45	20–25	Whole trees in motion and inconvenience felt when walking

point. This should prove to be a fairly painless exercise if you are using a mil dot or Map-Pro reticle, as they both offer multiple aim points for windage. The mil dot is a form of reticle that has dots on the windage and elevation cross-hairs (the dots being used as aim points and as a measuring device to calculate range).

Quite frankly, when hunting in the field where wind is obviously going to be a factor, the use of one of these reticle patterns is not only convenient but essential.

Adjusting windage with the cross-hairs can be done, but it takes a very accomplished marksman to do it. You can also dial in an adjustment for windage into the windage turret, but in order to do this you must have a broad range of settings relating to varying wind speeds, which takes a lot of time and patience on the range. So, you can see, the use of a mil dot or Map-Pro is the best option. The diagram on page 65 shows how to place the Map-Pro windage aim points in varying wind conditions.

The Map-Pro is designed to work with wind speeds up to a maximum of 18km/h (10mph).

If using a mil dot reticle, what you need to do is go to the range and set up a target of 30yd (27m). Aim at the bull with the centre of the cross-hairs and fire a shot; aim your next shot at the bull, using the first dot to the left of the centre cross, and continue shooting. Move on to the next dot after every shot until you run out of dots. Go down to the target and measure how far away the second shot is from the first, the third from the second, and so on. Write this information down. You now know how much compensation each mil dot offers.

There is no point in my writing down a list of measurements because these measurements will vary from gun to gun as a result of the weapon's individual trajectory and the type of ammunition used.

The next thing that you need to discover is how much your pellets get blown off line by a given wind speed. I would suggest a day when the wind is blowing at 9km/h (5mph) at 90 degrees.

Go to your range and fire at the bull using the centre of the cross-hairs; you should miss. If the wind is coming from the left, your shot should have been blown to the right. Go to

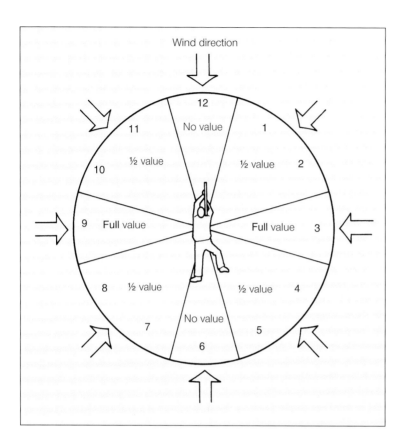

Wind wheel illustrating the impact of wind direction on the shooter.

the target and measure how far to the right the pellet has been blown, then fire a further two shots. Measure these also and take the average from the three measurements.

Let us say that your pellet is blown off target by 22mm. We now simply refer to our list of compensation measurements, which can be taped to the stock (for the more absent-minded, like me), or you could commit them to memory. Let us say that our first dot gives a compensation of 20mm, we then know that by using it as an aim point, placing the first dot on the bull, we will be just 2mm off target.

Don't forget that with wind coming from the left we would be using the first mil dot on the right; if the wind were coming from the right we would be using the mil dots on the left.

We can, with this information, now make calculations for other wind speeds. In our example, a 9km/h (5mph) wind blows the pellet 22mm off target, so a 4.5km/h (2½mph) wind

would blow the same pellet 11mm off target, and a 18km/h (10mph) wind 44mm off target. All the information we have acquired is specific to the range at which we set the target, in this case 30yd (27m). To get the compensation measurements for 25yd (23m) and 35yd (32m), we will have to set up targets at these ranges and go through the whole procedure again.

Learning, in this way, how your rifle behaves in different conditions is what makes the difference between a mediocre shot and a marksman.

MOUNTS, SCOPES AND RECOIL

The only real problem with telescopic sights is mounting them on the rifle. The mounts used to achieve this must be aligned with the utmost precision and the scope held with complete rigidity. The slightest play in the mounts will take the pellet dramatically off target.

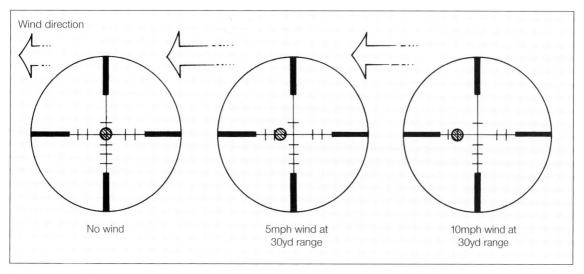

Wind direction

No wind

5mph wind at
30yd range

10mph wind at
30yd range

Compensating for varying crosswinds.

Play of as little as 0.25mm will take the pellet approximately 3cm (1½in) off target.

The problem of keeping the scope rigid is exacerbated by the vicious recoil action on spring-powered weapons. The recoil phase of a 12ft per lb spring-powered gun is even more violent in its effects upon a scope than that of a bullet gun. A spring-gun can literally shake the internals of a scope to pieces and vibrate the mounts until they're loose. To overcome this problem you need mounts of the highest quality.

I prefer to use two-piece mounts because they offer more adjustment than a one-piece mount, but they need to have two screws in the base and an arrestor pin in the rear mount. An arrestor pin is a screw with a point; it's positioned in the centre of the rear mount and can be tightened down so that it bites into the scope rail, giving additional grip.

The problem with screw-down arrestor pins is that they can vibrate loose: the violent recoil of the gun basically unscrews it. Sportsmatch, my preferred mounts, have overcome this problem by placing a fixed arrestor pin in the rear mount that cannot be vibrated loose, as it has no screw threads.

The pin needs to go into a pre-drilled hole in the scope rail; very few rifles have such a hole

so one needs to be drilled in the correct place. If you have a jig, and you know the anatomy of your gun very well, you could undertake the task yourself. If not, get a gunsmith to do it for you: they won't charge very much for drilling one hole.

The screw-down type of arrestor pin bites down fractionally into the scope rail, but the fixed arrestor pin sits deeply and snugly into the pre-drilled hole, providing a far better anchor than the screw-down variety. This is why the Sportsmatch mount is the best choice by far for a spring-powered weapon.

If you are fitting a Sportsmatch mount onto the rail of a PCP (in which case the arrestor pin is unnecessary), then simply knock the pin into the base of the mount using a wooden dowel and a rubber mallet.

You also need an arrestor block on the rail of a spring-powered rifle to prevent creep: rearwards movement. The BSA Lightning has one fitted as standard, but many rifles do not. If your spring-rifle does not have an arrestor block, it is well worth fitting one (they can be purchased relatively cheaply from Sportsmatch Mounts).

When selecting a scope for a spring-powered rifle, check to see that it is classified with a spring rating; if it is not it will be destroyed remarkably quickly. A spring-rated scope has specially strengthened internals to withstand the shock of the savage recoil, but I have in the past had spring-rated scopes, which, despite being designed to cope with the recoil of a spring-gun, lose their zero after a dozen or so shots. The internals in these scopes were not destroyed, it was just that the recoil managed to move them. This is most annoying and makes consistent shooting impossible. But I have been successful at stopping this from happening, by lining the scope mounts with a soft foam material (the underlay for wooden flooring is perfect). This acts as a damper, absorbing a large amount of the shock and softening it before it reaches the scope. Another thing worth considering is having the rifle tuned: a simple lubrication tuning will dramatically improve the weapon's handling, making it much smoother. Or you could have a custom-made spring and spring guide fitted, which will turn your rifle into an entirely different gun.

The .177 Lightning Tactical that I use had a recoil like an elephant gun. It soon shook the scopes off zero, so I padded the mounts out with two layers of foam, stripped the rifle down, and relubricated. It now shoots like a dream.

You will find that most rifles, even the very best, need some form of tinkering to get them right. That's because people are individuals and everybody has slightly different requirements. If your gun is not working correctly for you, figure out what is wrong and do something about it; if you can't, get someone to help you. Becoming a good shot is as much about getting your gun right, as it is about getting your technique right.

Good and Bad Mounts

It does not matter how much you spend on a scope, the thing will never work to its full potential until it is mounted on to quality mounts. When it comes to airgun mounts, there is only one company that I consider worth mentioning, and that is Sportsmatch.

In order for mounts to be effective, they must first fit the scope rail of the rifle – different rifles have different widthed scope rails so you need mounts that correspond to the width of your rail. There is no such thing as a standard rail, so there should be no such thing as a standard mount, but there is. Ignore such items and seek out a mount that was specifically manufactured to fit your rifle's rail.

Grip is everything in a mount. Their whole purpose in life is to hold rifle and scope together without losing its grip on either. In order to do this, the bottom of the base needs to have a good slope on it (*see* photo below) so that when the jaws are tightened together they close like the claws of an eagle.

Many mounts are made of poor-quality metal, so the jaws are soft and will soon wear, producing minute play in the mounts that will make consistent accuracy impossible. So make sure the mounts you choose are made from good-quality metal. This is difficult because poor-quality mounts are made to look like their superiors, but the difference can be felt in the weight. Mounts are obviously not heavy objects, but a good mount

Note the slope on the jaws of this Sportsmatch mount, which allows it to grip like a raptor.

should feel heavy for its size and seem substantial, whereas an inferior mount feels light and flimsy. Sportsmatch mounts have this substantial feel about them because they are made from the very finest materials.

Good-quality mounts will always have good-quality screws that look large and chunky. These screws are made from hardened metal so that the heads do not round off when tightened. On cheap mounts, when you tighten the jaws the screw heads round off making it impossible to apply any further tightening, resulting in the jaws never being brought fully home – which is fatal on a spring-powered weapon. There is nothing more annoying than having a screw head in the mount's base round off on you. I have in the past, on some mounts I was testing, had to drill out the screw heads because they became impossible to move. Quality screw heads, such as those used by Sportsmatch, will not round. Consequently, they enable you to really clamp down on the rail, gripping with such tenacity that a hammer wouldn't knock them off.

As far as air rifles go, I really think it is worth investing in a pair of Sportsmatch mounts. They may cost a little bit more but they will provide a perfect union between scope and rifle, which is essential if a decent level of marksmanship is to be achieved.

Mount Height
Mounts come in various heights: low, medium, and high. The height of the mount corresponds to the size of the scope's objective lens. The bigger the lens, the higher the scope will have to be mounted from the rifle. The following table shows the height of the mount required for the size of the objective lens.

Matching mounts to scope

Mount	Size of objective lens
Low	20–32mm
Medium	32–44mm
High	44–56mm

Low, medium and high mounts.

Never use a mount higher than you need to, as you want to keep the line of sight and the rifle's trajectory as close to one another as possible

The Most Advanced Mount
Sportsmatch have developed a fully adjustable scope mount that offers the shooter the most precise alignment of scope and rifle that it is possible to achieve, offering so many adjustments that every eventuality can be catered for.

State-of-the-art adjustable mounts from Sportsmatch.

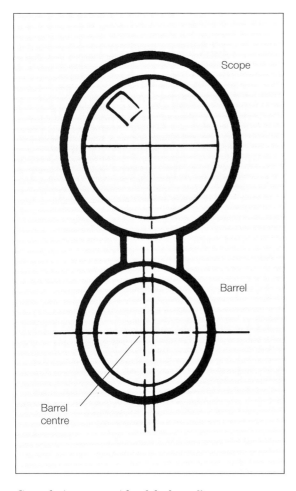

Scope

Barrel

Barrel
centre

Cross-hairs to one side of the barrel's centre.

This mount does not just hold the scope in place; it is actually used to zero in the scope. Rather than using the turrets to begin the zeroing process, you use the adjuster screws on the mount to begin. When zeroing with the turrets, you are moving the reticles inside the scope; but the scope itself stays stationary, whereas when zeroing with the adjustable mounts you are moving the actual position of the scope itself, so you can line it up with the centre of the barrel. You would be amazed how many scopes are actually set up to one side of the barrel.

With a low magnification scope set at ×1.5, you can often see by looking at the end of the

barrel, through the scope, that the vertical cross-hair actually sits to one side instead of aligned with the centre of the barrel. The Sportsmatch fully adjustable mounts allow you to align scope and barrel more precisely; they can facilitate this because the mounts are adjustable from side to side as well as up and down.

These mounts are more expensive than others, but if you can find the funds to afford a set you will be putting the most advanced mounts on the market onto your rifle. You will not regret it. These mounts are, in fact, so sought after that every time a new batch is manufactured they are sold out within days.

TYPES OF SCOPE

As far as hunting goes, there are only three main types of scope: the general-purpose; the low magnification close-range; and the long-range sniper-style scope. You can choose the scope that best suits your kind of shooting or, like me, you can have a selection of scopes to help to make your rig specific to the kind of shooting you are going to undertake on a given day.

Before examining the scopes in turn, it is worth mentioning that there are an awful lot of scope manufacturers to choose from. Far too many to mention them all. Some are very good and some not so good.

I use a range of scopes that come under the brand name Hawke. They manufacture high-quality optics specifically for use with air weapons. I favour the Hawke optics not only because they are extremely precise telescopic devices, with high-quality lenses that deliver a crystal clear image, but because the Hawke scopes are very tough pieces of equipment that will endure the most horrendous weather and the harshest of treatment. I have dropped my Hawke scopes, bashed them, neglected them, and even sat on one, and they still work perfectly.

Robustness is one of a scope's most important qualities. It is after all, not much good having high-quality optics if they can't endure

The Hawke Airmax scope.

the hunting environment of the British countryside. Some scopes are so delicate that if you sneeze you can upset them! I have broken no end of scopes in my time. Some may say that it is because I don't look after them properly. My defence is that hunting and pest control are very rough activities, and it is these activities that have broken the scopes, not my neglect.

I shall not mention the brand names of the scopes that have broken on me, some of them after a very short time, but I can tell you that the Hawke brand of scopes, which I now use exclusively, have never yet let me down.

The General-Purpose Scope

This kind of scope is most commonly found in the format 3–9×40. That means it has an adjustable magnification facility: from ×3 through to ×9, with an objective lens of 40mm, which will admit a large amount of light. The general-purpose scope is a jack of all trades, the lower end of the magnification being suitable for reasonably close-range work, the top end of the magnification scale being sufficient for long-range shots.

It must be borne in mind that the general-purpose scope is, by its very nature, a compromise. But having said that, many hunters

hunt their entire lives with nothing more than a moderately priced general-purpose scope, taking large bags and pulling off some very challenging shots.

My favourite general-purpose scope, which presently has teamed up with a .25 Lightning Tactical, is a new model, just released onto the market. It's the Hawke Airmax 4–12×40 AO, with Map 6 reticles, manufactured by a British company, Deben, as a specialist air rifle scope 4–12 means that it can be adjusted from four to twelve times magnification. This is, in my opinion, a much better set-up than 3–9×40.

Hawke Airmax gives you the extra three times magnification, which allows a much clearer picture for those long-range rabbit shots. The 40mm objective lens is more than big enough. Thanks to the extremely high-quality, fully multi-coated lenses used, this scope can cope well with low light conditions such as those experienced at dawn, dusk, and on cloudy days.

The ×4 magnification performs well enough at close-range, as the parallax is adjustable down to 10yd (9m), this means that the Airmax can engage targets as close as 30ft (9m). The Map 6 reticle (*see* diagram overleaf) is a pattern specifically designed for airgun

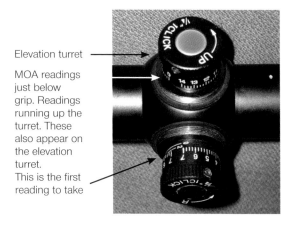

Elevation turret

MOA readings just below grip. Readings running up the turret. These also appear on the elevation turret.

This is the first reading to take

The turret markings on a Hawke Varmint scope.

elevation turrets until a 1in (25mm) grouping upon the bull is achieved. The marker below the centre cross will now be an accurate aim point for shots at 30yd (27m). You simply line this marker up with the target, rather than using the centre cross. This elevates the barrel giving you the increased distance required. The marker above the centre cross provides an accurate aim point for targets at 20yd (18m). This aim point is used to reduce the barrel elevation, thus reducing the range. This set up gives you the ability to accurately engage targets from 20 to 30yd (18 to 27m) without making any adjustments to the turrets, or having to make any calculations.

When engaging targets at close-range, you will need to reduce the level of magnification: ×12, down to ×4. You will also have to adjust the elevation turret, as the aim points must be re-zeroed to lower ranges. The centre cross must be changed from 25yd (23m) down to a 15yd (13m) zero. With a lot of general-purpose scopes, this involves removing a fiddly dust cap before you can get to the turret. But the Airmax does not have a dust cap on its

users and is exclusive to Deben. You will not find it in any other scopes. The cross-hairs on the Map 6 pattern offer a multiple selection of aim points that correspond to various distances.

I like to zero a general-purpose scope in at 25yd (23m). With the Airmax, this is done by lining up the centre of the cross-hairs on the target and adjusting the windage and

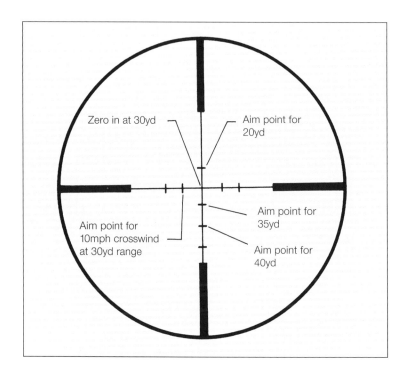

Zero in at 30yd

Aim point for 20yd

Aim point for 35yd

Aim point for 10mph crosswind at 30yd range

Aim point for 40yd

The Map 6 reticle.

elevation turret; instead it has what is known as an open-glove grip turret. That means that even when wearing thick winter gloves you can easily adjust this turret; also, there are a series of scales so that you can rapidly dial in the new setting with great precision.

Recording Range Settings
Once you have zeroed the Airmax in for 25yd (23m), write down the set-up by reading the markings coming up the turret, then the markings just below the grip. In my case, it gives a reading of 7/7.2. Now to find your zero for 15yd (13m).

Begin by reducing the magnification right down to ×4 and bring the parallax down from 25yd (23m) to 15yd (13m). Both these adjustments are simply made by rotating a ring. For the magnification, it is the power ring, for the parallax, the parallax ring. Next, zero the centre cross on a target positioned 15yd (13m) away from you. This should only require adjustments to the elevation turret to alter the angle of the barrel's elevation. The windage turret has to deal with crosswinds, so it should not need to be touched. Once you have a 1in (25mm) grouping at 15yd (13m) take a note of the set-up. The direction of rotation will be down, as you are zeroing to a closer-range. If you were zeroing to a more distant range, then it would be up. Now that the centre cross-hairs are zeroed at 15yd (13m), the aim point below the centre cross will be zeroed for use at 20yd (18m), the aim point above the centre cross will be zeroed for use at 10yd (9m). You now have a very precise selection of aim points for close-range work, from 10 to 20yd (9 to 18m).

To go back to the long-range set up, simply reverse the direction of the turret rotation and go up until you have the required setting. Turn the parallax ring back to 25yd (23m) and bring the magnification up to ×12. This adjustment will take all of five seconds.

Write down your long-range and short-range settings on a piece of paper, and tape them to your stock. You can now alternate between long- and short-range shooting with ease.

An awful lot of shooters are afraid to adjust the turrets once things are zeroed, fearing they will mess things up. But you should not fear the scope in this fashion: it is designed to be adjusted. If you are going to use it to its full potential you have to be able to adjust it quickly and with confidence. As long as you dial in accurate co-ordinates that you have worked out on the range, there should be no problem what so ever.

Close-range Scope
The close-range scope is a highly specialized piece of equipment and you only require one if you intend to work at very close-range. Essentially, there are only two types of shooting that require this kind of scope: rat and feral pigeon shooting.

A close-range scope has lower magnification and a smaller objective lens than you would find on a general-purpose scope, the usual specification being 1.5–5×20. That means that the scope has an adjustable magnification from ×1.5 to ×5, and an objective lens of 20mm.

There are two reasons for the low magnification. Firstly, the close-range hunter can often be taking targets measured in feet rather than yards. I know from my own hunting experiences with feral pigeons, that targets 10ft (3.5m) away are not uncommon, even 5ft (1.5m) on occasions. You simply would not be

The Hawke Nite Eye Scope.

able to focus on such targets with a high magnification, for such close work a scope needs to come right down to ×1.5, much more than this just produces a blur.

The second reason has to do with the nature of close-range quarry. Rats are very active, rarely staying still for two seconds together; pigeons can be presented as a moving target as they walk back and forth along the rafters looking down at you. Rats and feral pigeons present themselves as a target for only a very limited amount of time, seconds at best. One second there is a target, the next there is none. To engage such targets humanely and successfully, you need a scope that can facilitate rapid target acquisition.

To tackle moving targets you need a scope that can be used to track movement. Both these requirements are met by low magnification because low magnification gives a wide field of view. What does that mean?

With a high magnification scope, what you see through the lenses is the kill zone of the target and very little else. If the target moves very slightly it disappears from the scope's field of view. With a low magnification scope, you get to see the target and quite a lot of the area surrounding it. The target viewed through a low magnification scope can move some distance and still remain in the scope's field of view.

When you step into a barn full of feral pigeons, they will wait a second or two before taking flight, showering you with feathers in the process. With a high magnification scope, you would fix it on the rafters and, because of its narrow field of view, you will see only one pigeon – and that's if you're very lucky. You'll most likely end up looking at a vacant piece of rafter, so you have to search for a target. If you move left the pigeon will probably be to your right, but before you have realized this they will all have gone.

With a low magnification scope you would point it at the rafters and the wide field of view will present you with a number of targets. All you have to do is select the one you want and take it down. The magnification scope with

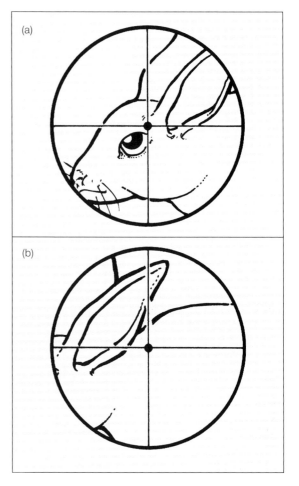

Field of view for high magnification scope. (a) Cross-hairs on kill zone. (b) Tiniest movement from the rabbit removes the cross-hairs from the kill zone.

its wide field of view thus offers near instantaneous target acquisition. The lower the magnification the wider the field of view, so a magnification of only 1.5 is what you want for rapid target acquisition. On moving targets (by that I refer to slow-moving targets – feral pigeons and rats – not fast-moving targets such as rabbits) with a high magnification scope, you will always be chasing the target and, if you do eventually get your cross-hairs onto it, it will have stepped out of view before you can pull the trigger.

With a low magnification scope the wide field of view enables you to see in which

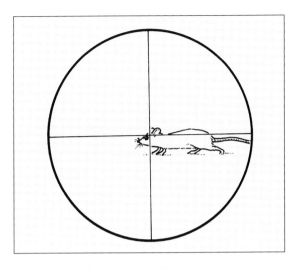

Field of view for low magnification scope.

and down a rafter, or a rat searching for food, it is acceptable to engage them at close-range. I think a .25 weapon is best suited for such a task as it allows for a body shot, which gives the moving target a larger kill zone.

That well-known airgun hunter of the 1980s, John Darling, used to engage fast-moving rabbits which he took down successfully with a head shot. Such shooting requires an exceptionally high level of skill and alertness, and is not something that everybody should try. Andrew George Elliot, in his book *Gun Fun and Hints* (Elliot Right Way Books), records shooting crows in flight with an airgun, though he brought down only a quarter of those he shot at. An airgun in skilled hands can take a moving target, but to ensure an ethically justifiable shot, only slow-moving targets should be taken with a low magnification scope.

My favourite low magnification scope is the Hawke Nite Eye, illuminated dot reticle in 1.5–6×44 format. This scope has an adjustable magnification, beginning at ×1.5 and going up to ×6; the objective lens is 44mm. This is quite a large lens for a close-range scope, the advantage being that it admits a larger degree of light than you would get with a smaller lens, allowing the scope to be employed in low-light conditions.

I have managed to use this scope against feral pigeons in a feed shed, shooting into the dimly lit rafters where I would need a light

direction the quarry is moving so you can follow it, the scope's field of view always staying slightly ahead of the quarry's movements. With this kind of scope you can use a technique for engaging moving targets, where you move your aim point ahead of the target, setting it at a site where you expect the target to appear. Then when the quarry moves to that location bringing itself in line with your aim point, you squeeze the trigger.

I know that airgun hunting by the nature of its power limitations, is mainly confined to the taking of static targets. But when the target is slow-moving like a pigeon, sauntering up

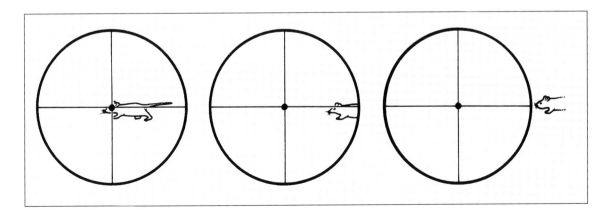

Placing aim point ahead of target allowing the quarry to walk on to it.

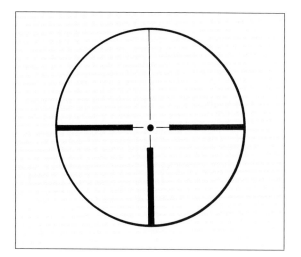

30/30 Dot reticle.

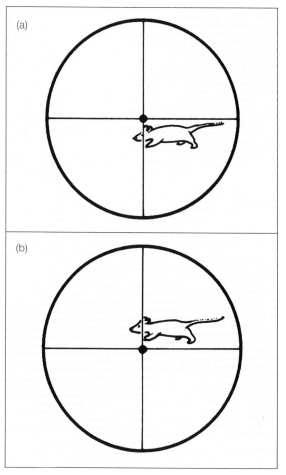

Placing the aim point. (a) Holding above for long-range shots. (b) Holding below for close-range shots.

source to use other scopes. The Nite Eye has a dot reticle based on the 30/30 pattern. The dot at the centre of the cross-hairs is the quickest of all aim points, allowing for very rapid target acquisition. It takes the eye and brain less time to train a dot on the kill zone, than it does to align cross-hairs or any other form of reticle.

This is why military weapons designed for close-quarters fighting are fitted with a scope that has a dot reticle. The fact that the dot can be illuminated on the Nite Eye, offering eleven different levels of brightness, makes it extremely viable in low-light conditions, the dot vividly contrasting with the target.

Using black cross-hairs, or even a black dot when they are placed against a target in a dull setting, the reticles merge with the target until they are almost invisible, and it becomes next to impossible to line up the aim point with the kill zone. The illuminated dot sits on top of the target, sticking out like a sore thumb, allowing the aim point and the kill zone to be easily differentiated and lined up, making this the perfect scope for serious pest control operatives.

I zero my close-range scope in at 15yd (13m); for targets below or above this range I employ a hold-off system. Which means that instead of aiming the aim point directly at the

kill zone, I aim above or below it according to the range. Learning how far above or below a target to place the aim point is a skill that is acquired on the range. Zero your rifle in at 15yd (13m), then practise on 10 and 20yd (9 and 18m) targets, learning how much hold-off is required to achieve the necessary trajectory. Before leaving low magnification and close-range scopes, I should mention that when you have the scope set on the low end of the magnification scale, ×1.5 through to ×2, you will when looking through the scope see the end of your rifle's barrel. This is quite normal and is the result of the scope's wide field of view, when you go up to ×2.5 the barrel will no longer be in view.

If your barrel is nice and shiny, it will act like a mirror, throwing up a strong glare that will distract your eye. To overcome this you need to dull down the end of the barrel. There are neoprene covers that can be slipped over the silencer, or you could use camouflage tape, but I cover the end of my rifle's barrel with a piece of rawhide, held in place with electrical tape.

Long-Range Scope

This is a scope with a very high level of magnification; the usual format is 6–24×44, meaning that the scope has adjustable magnification beginning at ×6 and going up to a whopping ×24, the objective lens is 44mm.

My personal favourite in this format, and one of the very finest scopes on the market is the Hawke Varmint. A specialist long-range scope that can be used at distances in excess of 30yd (27m) with the right kind of weapon. The whole point of using a scope like this, is to enhance the target as much as possible so that you can clearly see the position of the aim point in relation to the animal's kill zone. For this you select the highest magnification setting possible.

I find that with the Varmint, at ranges from 20 to 35yd (18 to 32m), ×20 is the best setting.

The Hawke Varmint scope.

You can go as high as ×24, but the target does begin to blur at the edges with such a high level of magnification. In order to use magnification of this magnitude, you will need to have a steadfast support for the rifle. I always use a Polecat tripod when using a long-range scope. The huge level of magnification not only magnifies the target, it magnifies the shooter's wobble.

A lot of shooters say that a high magnification scope increases the level of their wobble. It doesn't. However, what it does do is increase your perception of your wobble. It's just like the rabbit's head, its head hasn't actually got any bigger, it's just your perception, due to magnification, of it that's got bigger. If you don't have a well-supported firing position with high magnification, the reticle will literally wobble about like a jelly.

One of the biggest problems the airgun shooter has with a high magnification scope like this is that it was designed to work at ranges way beyond the capability of an airgun. As a result there is not sufficient adjustment in the elevation turret, which means that you might be shooting several inches over the top of the target. To counter this you need to increase the height between the scope and the rifle. There are two ways to do this: the DIY approach, or the very professional approach. For the DIY approach, place several layers of foam material in the bottom section of the scope mounts, underneath the scope – the foam used beneath wooden flooring is ideal for this. For the professional approach, purchase a high-tech, adjustable mount that can increase its height. The lower part of the mounts, into which the scope body tube sits, screws up or down.

The Varmint has what is known as a Mil Dot reticle (*see* diagram overleaf). The vertical and horizontal cross-hairs on this reticle have a number of black dots spaced along them, thus giving you a selection of aim points.

How you use these dots is as follows: set the magnification ring to the magnification of your choice (mine is ×20), then zero in with the centre cross on a target at 30yd (27m)

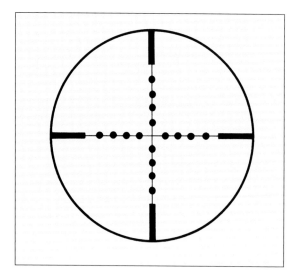

Mil Dot reticle.

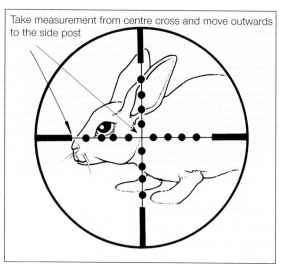

Measuring with the Mil Dot reticle at ×20 magnification. This rabbit is at approximately 30yd.

distance. Then set up a target at 25yd (23m), use the first dot below the centre cross, and see where this places you on the target. If it doesn't land on target, keep experimenting with the dots below the centre cross until you find an aim point that brings you on target. Now move the target out to 35yd (32m) and do the same again, only this time use the dots above the centre cross.

The Mil Dot reticle can also be used for range-finding, by carrying out certain calculations in relation to the size of the target as measured between the dots. However, I find that by the time my mind has carried out the required calculations, the rabbit is on to me and has packed up and hopped off. I have however devised a more rapid way of using the dots for approximate range-finding. If I view a rabbit through a scope set at ×20 magnification, and the distance between the back of its eye and the base of its ear is a distance of two dots measured from the centre cross to an outer post, then I know the rabbit is approximately 30yd (27m) away. If the same measurement is three dots then I know that the rabbit is

approximately 20yd (18m) away. With these two simple measurements to guide me, I am able to make a pretty accurate assessment of range. If the measurement is a bit less than three dots, I know that the rabbit is likely to be 25yd (23m) away; if it measures a bit less than two dots, I know it is more likely to be 35yd (32m) away.

You will have to make precise calculations for yourself on your range, as the measurement varies according to the degree of magnification used. Set up a life-size target (*see* Appendix II) at 30yd (27m), measure the distance between the back of the rabbit's eye and the base of its ear, using the centre cross and moving to an outer post. When you have a measurement, which may be two dots, two and a half dots, or one and a half dots, commit that measurement to memory and you have a means of identifying a 30yd (27m) target. Do the same at 20yd (18m).

If you wish to make a measurement at a lower magnification, say ×12, you will need to use more length across the horizontal reticle, going from the side post of one side and measuring across.

Long Range Scope
Suitable For Lamping

A lot of shooters just use their standard general-purpose scope for lamping and manage to achieve acceptable results. But if you want to up the ante for yourself, get a scope that has been specially designed to operate in low-light conditions. Such scopes have a huge objective lens, usually 50mm, which allows the scope to gather a large amount of light.

Shooting at night, in lamplight, the difference between a 40mm and a 50mm objective lens becomes obvious in the clarity of the image that the shooter is able to see. My favourite lamping scope is the Hawke Map-Pro reticle pattern No. 6, which is specifically designed for airgun use.

I use a Map-Pro with the following specification: 4–16×50 AO. For lamping purposes, I dial the magnification ring right up to the maximum ×16 and have the parallax set on 30yd (27m). The only problem with a 50mm objective lens is fitting the scope to the rifle: the lens is so wide that you require specially designed high mounts to give sufficient clearance between rifle and scope. I have seen 50mm objective scopes fitted so close to the rifle, that the parallax ring would not rotate as it was jammed against the rifle. Though you want to raise the scope sufficiently to clear the rifle, you do not want to raise it any higher than absolutely necessary. The greater

The Hawke Map-Pro scope.

the difference between the line of sight and the barrel, the greater the degree of difficulty involved in calibrating them to work in unity. For this reason, the best mounts to use are height-adjustable mounts so that they can be set at exactly the right height, not too low and not too high. The Map-Pro reticle pattern No. 6, offers the shooter a variety of aim points if the scope is used at ×6 magnification; magnification above or below ×6 will present a different set-up altogether. All you have to do is zero the scope in, using the centre cross at 30yd (27m) at ×6 magnification; the other aim points will be zeroed into the distances specified in the diagram on page 70.

CHAPTER FOUR

Ethical Aspects of Air Rifle Hunting

HARVESTING QUARRY AT THE RIGHT TIME

I know of plenty of shooters who have scant regard for the quarry they hunt, shooting anything that moves. I recall a gamekeeper who shot a rabbit simply to check that his rifle was correctly zeroed; he did not go and collect the shot rabbit to use it in any way; he just killed

Rabbits harvested from the wild, and hung – waiting to be butchered.

for the heck of it. Such an attitude is sadly not the rarity it should be.

As a shooter you should adopt an ethical approach and respect the quarry you hunt. Far from having a mind to destroy every rabbit and pigeon you see, you should have the mind of a conservationist, doing the utmost to sustain a healthy population of rabbit, pigeon and carrion on your ground.

I know shooters who shoot every jackdaw they see, even when there are very few on the shooting ground. They say that the killing of all the jackdaws allows the songbirds to breed without having their eggs destroyed. But let us not forget that the jackdaw, like every other animal in nature, has a role to play. So, although an over-abundance of jackdaws on your shooting ground may affect songbirds, this is not the case where the numbers are well balanced by a selective shooting policy.

As a shooter you should know how large the population is of all the quarry species, and take out only that which needs to be taken out to keep things in balance. The law does not allow you to kill birds of any variety unless they are present in pest proportions. Half a dozen jackdaws on a hundred acres of farm land is nowhere near pest proportions, so to take them would be outside the bounds of the law.

Your role as a hunter is to manage ground, not decimate it like a vandal horde. You must never just shoot something for the fun of it. There must always be purpose and reason behind each and every shot you take, or ethically you do not have a leg to stand on.

If you think that the farmers who own the land you shoot on would never wear such an approach, then think again. I shoot over many thousands of acres, and all the farmers I deal with are more than happy with my policy. It is in tune with the present agricultural policy, which leans towards the management of the land as a natural habitat.

My main quarry is the rabbit. But during the summer months, when they are engaged in the conception and raising of young, I choose, on ethical and conservation grounds, not to hunt them.

There are a number of factors that have made me adopt this approach. Firstly, I am not willing to risk killing milky does that have a litter of dependent kits relying on her for nourishment. Lining up the cross-hairs on a milky doe does not just kill one rabbit but as many as twelve: the first rabbit will have died instantly, but the other eleven will starve to death over a period of many hours. This is not only cruel but very short-sighted. If the doe is left alone to raise her litter, that litter when grown will increase the rabbit population on your ground, offering large bags and more sport during the winter months. Some hunters will tell you that the farmers will not tolerate such an approach, but that is not my experience. As a smallholder I live and work among farmers, and not one of them has asked me to eradicate the rabbits on their ground. They simply want them managed by somebody who knows what they are doing. If you eradicate the rabbits on a farm you not only deprive yourself of a valuable shooting ground, you also upset the balance of the ecosystem. No rabbits mean no birds of prey, no rabbits mean that the fox has to look closer to the farm for his food, no rabbits mean no stoats, and no rabbits mean that the marginal ground on the farm is not grazed.

As shooters we have to realize that our actions reach far beyond the death of a rabbit or bird. We can, and do, change the face of the countryside and if we are not well-informed naturalists, that change can be detrimental.

As a smallholder I realize the importance of working with nature. If I continually plant up a patch of ground without giving it a period of rest, it will become exhausted, not having sufficient nutrients left in it to yield a crop. Rabbits (and all other quarry species with the exception of rats and feral pigeons which have to be completely eradicated) should be seen in the same way, as a valuable crop. If you do not give them a rest, by laying down your gun during the breeding season, the rabbit population will become exhausted and your harvest depleted.

A good hunter is, above all else, a conservationist. Your job is to manage a healthy population of rabbits, not too big and not too small. To do this, you need to understand your quarry inside out so that you can recognize the factors on your ground that will affect the rabbit population: climate, disease and predation.

Shooting is so much more that just being good with a gun. It's about becoming part of the countryside, so that you can see and feel and smell what is going on around you. As you go across your ground on hunting trips, you should be checking on things by reading the signs. Is the fox or badger busy upon your ground? The runs, droppings, and evidence of kills are all there for you to see, if you look. By assessing the hunting patterns of predators you can judge the size of bag you should be taking off the ground. If predation is very high, you should decrease your bag; if predation is low you should increase your bag. Working in tune with nature like this is the mark of a good hunter, not how many rabbits you manage to put in the bag.

I have known people boast about a brilliant shoot where they took forty rabbits in a single night with the lamp. On the next trip they took twenty and finally they took ten. The person then comes up to me and says that all the rabbits have suddenly disappeared. In just two weeks they have managed to destroy a rabbit population, ruining what could have been a brilliant shoot.

Greed is the shooter's greatest enemy. Even the enormous herds of buffalo that roamed the American West were brought to extinction by greedy hunters. The American Indians had skilfully harvested the buffalo for thousands of years, until greed came with powerful long-range rifles that allowed whole herds to be slaughtered in one afternoon. In Canada, greed brought the beaver to the edge of extinction as trappers, ignorant of the impact of their actions, pursued their quarry until the beaver could not breed sufficient offspring to offset the losses they were suffering.

In Pembrokeshire, before the introduction of myxomatosis, there were hundreds of thousands if not millions of rabbits, skilfully managed by the Pembrokeshire warreners who used to earn a handsome living from rabbit catching. These men knew how to harvest a rabbit crop so that it flourished – even though the harvest was large. We can learn a lot from the approach taken by the Pembrokeshire warreners.

Some shooters may say they only shoot bucks (male rabbits) during the breeding season. It is perfectly possible for a shooter with a good knowledge of rabbit morphology to tell the difference between a buck and a doe by the shape of the head, but taking the bucks can lead to serious problems. There are, for obvious reasons, fewer bucks than does. By removing large numbers of bucks during the breeding season, you can have a dramatic and detrimental effect on a colony's ability to rejuvenate itself. Does cannot reproduce by themselves and so a healthy number of bucks is required.

Not only does summer rabbit shooting have a detrimental effect on rabbit populations, it is unproductive as summer rabbits do not make the best eating. Though the grass and herbage are at their most vital during the summer months, being packed full of sugars, the doe is constantly pregnant (she can in fact be carrying a litter whilst still suckling another), so all the nutrition she takes in is drained away to support her offspring. The doe also has chemical changes taking place in her body, which affects the flavour of the meat. Bucks are also at their leanest during the summer time, becoming rakish just like dogs that are around bitches on heat.

The summer affects not only the quality and the quantity of the meat but the pelts. The doe is constantly pulling lumps of fur from her coat to line her nest, making her a very shabby specimen indeed, and the buck is always fighting, which leads to his coat getting badly damaged. Besides this, the lush winter coat has been shed for a much thinner summer one. Just as I would not pick a strawberry when it was still green, I do not shoot summer rabbit because they are not ripe for the taking. I truly believe that the most sensible approach when it comes to rabbits is to hang up your gun from the months of May to September.

The strategy I have laid out here for hunting rabbits can be applied to other quarry species – with the exception of large infestations of rats and feral pigeons (because of the diseases they can spread). Having said this, I will not shoot hen birds that are tending squabs (the young); neither will I shoot the squabs themselves. There is something distasteful and unethical to my mind about killing an animal or bird that is tending young. I leave nesting areas entirely alone, and concentrate my efforts on adults that do not have young. Some pest controllers will shoot anything: squabs, the birds tending them, infant rabbits hardly the size of a man's clenched fist. I will not.

CARE OF YOUR QUARRY

Lots of people who don't shoot think that someone like me must truly loathe rabbits because I hunt them with such ardour. They could not be further from the truth. I have a real admiration and liking for rabbits. To my mind they are one of the nation's most important and endearing mammals, and far from killing every rabbit I come across I quite often intervene to help them.

One day I happened to spot a rabbit kit (immature rabbit) slap bang in the middle of the road. Other motorists drove straight over the top of it but I stopped, scooped up the

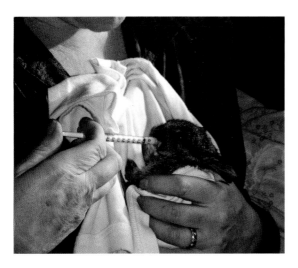

My mother tending an injured rabbit kit.

petrified little creature and took it home, not for the pot but to be fostered. As soon as I arrived home I handed the tiny bundle of fur over to mother, as she is the expert at raising orphans having had considerable success in the field. She used a syringe to give the kit regular offerings of goat's milk. When the rabbit was big and strong enough to return to the wild it was released.

If I ever spot a rabbit with myxomatosis, I catch the pathetic creature, which is not difficult, and put it out of its misery. I then dispose of the carcass in such a way that it cannot infect other rabbits, which means burning or burying the body. The myxovirus can devastate a rabbit population. If it shows its ugly head on your shooting ground, you will need to make daily visits to cull out and bury any infected rabbits that you come across. If you are very diligent, you may be able to stop the disgusting disease from totally destroying your shoot.

But remember, whilst the rabbit population is recovering from the impact of the disease you will have to reduce, or more likely cease, your shooting activities altogether for a while. Caring for the quarry on your ground in this way is what can turn a moderate shooting ground into a great one.

INJURED QUARRY

One of the worst things the hunter can ever experience is the sight of a wounded rabbit, bird or even rat crawling away to die slowly and very painfully. Hopefully this won't happen to you too often but, sooner or later, no matter how good you are, you will make a mistake. The pellet will miss the point of aim and cause an injury.

I remember an awful incident last year when I was out lamping. I had my scope lined up superbly on a big rabbit in the middle of a field; it wasn't a very difficult shot and success was all but guaranteed, yet when I squeezed the trigger I felt a sudden jerk backwards as one of the young heifers that was being grazed in the field grabbed the strap of my game bag and pulled me so violently that I nearly fell over.

The heifer meant no harm; she just thought there might be something in the bag to eat. I gave the heifer a gentle elbow in the snout, which made her let go and when I looked back at the rabbit, which should have been lying dead, I saw the most pitiful sight. The rabbit was going round and round in tiny circles, its head tilted in an odd fashion to one side. My shot had somehow disrupted the rabbit's sense of balance. I have seen some horrible sights, but never have I seen an animal more distressed. I cocked my rifle, dropped to one knee and aimed a shot for the chest.

The rifle I was using was very powerful. I was under 30yd (27m) and a head shot would have been difficult, so the body was the only sensible target. The second shot thankfully knocked the rabbit to the ground, and it was dead in seconds. Injuring an animal in this way is, for any decent human being, traumatic and has been known to put some people off shooting for life, so be prepared.

If you injure an animal or bird and it crawls away into cover, you are ethically obliged to do everything in your power to track that animal down and bring its misery, which you have caused, to an end. Some shooters just walk away in search of their next victim. This is unforgivable.

Tracking Down Injured Quarry

You make a shot that goes wrong for some reason and you injure your quarry, which crawls away into thick cover before you can deliver a second shot. What do you do about it?

First make a mental note of where the quarry entered the undergrowth, then slowly head for that point; don't rush or make too much noise. Tread very softly, as the injured animal could be lying only feet away from where it entered the undergrowth. When you reach the point at which the quarry entered, crouch down and look for any signs of activity: blood or feathers, trampled-down grass that might indicate which direction the animal took.

You now have to use your knowledge of your quarry (which should be considerable as the result of hours studying their behaviour patterns, both in the field and at home with your head in books on natural history) and look around for the most obvious hiding place. It could take a considerable time to search out that hiding place; in fact, it may take the entire time you have allotted for that shoot. Nevertheless, it is your ethical duty to do everything humanely possible to find the animal you have injured.

The ability to read tracks may well prove useful when going after injured quarry, but more often that not, the ground is too well covered in vegetation to take tracks. However, in muddy conditions, or in the snow, a trail may well be left. So study the prints left behind by different animals until they are familiar and identifiable to you.

I have another weapon in my armoury for the locating of injured quarry, which rapidly speeds up the process of finding the animal. (The quicker you find the injured quarry, the less time it has to suffer.) That weapon is a big lump of a collie dog, by the name of Pilot. He is a highly trained hunting dog, and, among his other skills, he has been trained to track animals. I call him a hunting dog because he has so many functions that to simply call him a tracker would not fully describe his role. When out ferreting he drives rabbits below ground, so they can be bolted into nets by the ferrets. He can also locate rabbits below ground (those that the ferrets have killed), showing me where to dig. Pilot can also be used to find quarry: if

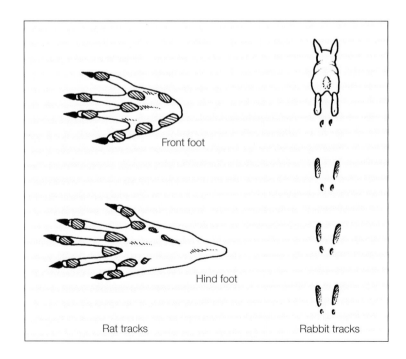

Front foot

Hind foot

Rat tracks

Rabbit tracks

The ability to read tracks may be useful when following quarry.

Pilot, one of my specially trained tracking dogs.

there is a single rabbit on a hundred acres of ground he can find it.

When required to track, I simply show him the point at which the animal entered the undergrowth, tell him to find, and away he goes into the undergrowth. Moments later he has cornered or grabbed the quarry.

Training a dog to track in this way is not an easy undertaking – whole books have been written on the subject – but if you have (or can acquire) the skill to do it it is well worthwhile.

Dispatching Injured Quarry

When injured quarry is found and retrieved it has to be dispatched. Many years ago, I was beating through a field of sugarbeet when a beater, eight down the line from me, came across an injured partridge. He picked it up, but didn't know how to dispatch the poor suffering creature, so passed it down the line to the next man until it came to me. Not one of them knew what to do. I broke its neck, ending its suffering.

If you are going to shoot you must know how to kill – not just with a gun but with your bare hands. As someone considering taking up this sport you need to decide whether or not you have the stomach for dispatching injured quarry. If the answer to that is no, be assured there is no shame in it. Some people have the stomach for killing, others do not; and others can do it so coldly that it's disturbing.

Dispatching Rabbits

As a busy ferreter I am something of an expert at dispatching rabbits. I have killed thousands of them over the years with my hands – quickly, efficiently, and humanely. The method I use is called the chop and is by far the easiest method for the beginner to learn.

Some sportsmen prefer to break the rabbit's neck, either by tilting it backwards or rotating the head until the neck snaps. This is a humane method in the hands of an expert, but if you hesitate or blunder you can cause a terrible amount of distress, dangling the rabbit between life and death. If you do not break the neck cleanly, you will have a rabbit that is paralysed rather than dead.

The chop is simply the delivery of a karate-style blow with the edge of the hand to the base of the rabbit's skull. This separates the cervical vertebrae, causing instant, painless death.

1. Pick up the injured rabbit by the loins.
   Do not under any circumstances pick up the rabbit by the hind legs: it will jerk its body back and forth with tremendously powerful movements that may cause you to lose your grip; more importantly these jerking movements will cause the injured rabbit to suffer unnecessary pain. If you touch its tail or hind legs you get kicked;

if you touch its face you can get bitten or scratched by the front claws.

Rabbits picked up by the hind legs will always struggle, but rabbits picked up by the loins will go limp. Foxes and dogs pick up rabbits by the loins, and when taken in this way the rabbit seems to know that its fate is sealed and it gives in to the inevitable. Having said that, a seized rabbit will sometimes let out the most almighty ear-piercing squeal that goes right through you. I am not sure whether this noise comes from sheer panic or whether it is a warning to other rabbits of danger. (A dying rat will nobly warn others in its colony that danger is at hand. I tend to think that the rabbit squeal has something of this nature about it.)

2. Now that you have the rabbit firmly by the loins, hold it across your body, head down in front of you. Tense the fingers of the striking hand (keeping the thumb firmly pressed up against your forefinger so that you have an inflexible weapon like a plank of wood). The part of the hand with which you strike the rabbit is the lower fleshy portion below the little finger; do not use the fingers. If you strike it with the fingers you may well kill the rabbit, but you will also bruise your fingers. You need to aim your strike at the base of the rabbit's skull, the point where the head meets the neck. The chop is not a downward motion striking the top of the neck, but a forward motion striking the back of the head and forcing it forward, pulling the cervical vertebrae apart and causing severe haemorrhaging. Do not try to get your blow under the rabbit's ears, if they should be pressed down against the rabbit's neck simply make the blow on top of them.

Do not start your blow from too far away. Making a blow of this nature from feet away at such a small target takes the considerable skill of experienced ferreters or martial artists. Most people would miss from such a distance, going clean over the top of the rabbit's head. I have seen

it done – missing the rabbit's head and striking themselves with a severe blow to the leg. The blow needs to come from a distance of about 4–6in (10–15cm). Hold the hand at that distance, then draw it back slightly at the fingertips until they are almost horizontal, then strike with a swift powerful blow.

A second blow may be required by the inexperienced practitioner, but don't worry if that is the case – the first blow will have knocked the rabbit out cold. If the rabbit does not twitch (all rabbits twitch when they die), then it is not dead, merely knocked out, and a second blow is required.

Dispatching Birds

For the dispatching of birds I recommend the purchase of a dispatching tool. It looks like a pair of pliers and is used to break the bird's neck. I recommend the use of such a tool, as the killing of a bird by hand involves wringing its neck, literally twisting the neck until it snaps. The risk with this is that you may twist too far, pulling the head off and revealing a bloody, twitching, neck stump. A lot of people do not have the stomach for such a sight, besides which, the bloody stump makes an awful mess in the game bag. My advice is to use a dispatching tool which will ensure a clean, bloodless kill.

The bird, once its neck is broken, will flap about furiously so make sure you hold the wings down.

Dispatching Rats

Never, under any circumstances, pick up an injured rat. A rat will, despite some tall tales to the contrary, always run away from human beings if possible. However, if cornered they are likely to attack. A rat is not a tiger and will not kill; but a rat bite is a very nasty injury, not just because of the amount of tissue damage but because of the potential for serious, and possibly life-threatening, infection.

When you have shot a rat, make doubly sure it is dead before you pick it up. If you have injured a rat you have an ethical responsibility to bring the creature's suffering to a rapid end. However much they may be despised by man they feel pain just like birds and rabbits, so they must be brought to a quick end.

The best way to deal with an injured rat is, if possible, to shoot it again; the only problem with this strategy is you may miss. You can dispatch an injured rat with a point-blank range shot, but this can be dangerous.

I am quite happy to use a .25 at point-blank range as the .25 pellet, even at this range, distorts dramatically and loses all its energy so stays inside the rat. Other calibres are more than likely to go in one side and come flying out the other, with sufficient energy left in them to cause a wicked ricochet that could easily destroy an eye, so always think twice about shooting at point-blank range.

The other way to dispatch an injured rat that is unable to move or can only move slowly, is to stamp on the head. It is a very effective method that causes instantaneous death. Some martial arts have a stamp technique that will kill a human being, so you can imagine the result of stamping on a rat.

SAFETY

Some of you might be thinking that this subject has landed up in the wrong chapter. Surely safety is not an ethical issue? Ethics are the possession of a responsible individual who has the ability to distinguish right behaviour from wrong. Therefore, they do what is right because they feel morally obligated. Safety is right behaviour that should be practised as a result of a moral obligation to the welfare of others. So it fits very well into this chapter on ethics.

You may think that I am overdoing it, but consider for a moment the plight of a small girl who picked up her father's loaded air rifle, which had not been put in a safe place, and pointed it at her sister. With no sense of malice, she pulled the trigger. Either the safety catch was not applied or it was knocked off as the child played with the weapon. Either way, the pellet shot through the air at a range of a few

yards, struck the sister, pierced her skull and lodged in her brain – where it remains as it is in such a position that it is too dangerous to attempt to remove it. The effect a pellet will have upon the brain, is at present, unclear.

The incident I mention here is not an isolated case. It is one of the reasons why I believe that any one wishing to own a weapon of any kind, whether it be a shotgun, firearm or air rifle, should have to attend a mandatory course on gun handling safety. You cannot drive a car unless you first pass a fairly comprehensive test, yet you can own a lethal weapon without having to pass any test whatsoever. Madness.

Many airgunners strenuously object to attempts to make the ownership of airguns more restrictive. There are, at the time of writing, proposals afoot in Scotland for a ban on the general sale of air weapons, making their purchase available only to licensed individuals. This has got many airgun users up in arms, but not me. The proposal was put forward because a little boy of just two years old was shot to death by a man using an air rifle to commit a deliberate act of murder, for which he is now serving a life sentence. If licensing airgun users can help to prevent another death, and the evidence seems to suggest that it will, then it should be supported by airgun shooters.

If we have a legitimate reason for using air rifles, then why should we fear being licensed? Deer stalkers have to be licensed to use a firearm; it does not stop them pursuing their sport. Wildfowlers have to be licensed to use a shotgun, and it does not stop them pursuing their sport. So why should licensing stop us pursuing ours? There are millions of air rifles in circulation, but no records of who owns these weapons or what they are being used for. A large number of rifles are in the hands of irresponsible people, as is evidenced by the many incidents of firemen being shot and injured with air weapons, even when dealing with emergencies. Countless numbers of pets are injured every year by cold-hearted individuals. The Cats' Protection League recorded 100,000 cat injures over the course of a year caused by airgun pellets. Such travesties need to be stopped, and licensing airgun shooters may just do it.

Those airgun users who feel their civil liberties will be infringed by licensing are actually helping to throw an umbrella of protection over those who misuse airguns. We, as responsible airgun users, should be in the vanguard of tackling the dangerous and illegal use of air weapons for the good of the sport and, more importantly, for the protection of others.

Safety Procedures

Never under any circumstances point a weapon at somebody whether it be loaded or not.

Whenever you pick up a weapon, make it a habit to check that the safety catch is engaged, then inspect to see if the weapon is loaded. With a spring-powered weapon, open the barrel slightly (there is no need to compress the spring) and peer down the barrel; if you can see daylight then the weapon is not loaded. With a PCP remove the magazine, tilt the gun and look into the barrel, you should be able to see the skirt of a pellet if there is one centred in the barrel. If you are unsure return the bolt or lever, point the gun in a safe direction and squeeze the trigger.

With a PCP, removing the magazine usually involves cocking the weapon. With the magazine gone, the weapon is not able to discharge a pellet but the trigger is set, ready to release a pulse of air when it is depressed, so to make the gun truly safe the trigger should be released. Do this by returning the bolt or lever, removing the safety catch, and depressing the trigger; this is referred to as dry-firing and does not damage PCPs. Dry-firing a spring-powered weapon can do serious damage to the internal components, so never dry-fire a spring-gun.

When handing a weapon to another person, pass it butt-first with the barrel facing the ground. If the ground happens to be concrete or a similar hard surface, pass the weapon butt-first but with the barrel pointing up in the air. When you take a gun from another person, even if you have witnessed them make

the gun safe, check it yourself. The gun is now your responsibility, so if anything goes wrong it's your fault as the gun is in your hands. Check it.

When you have finished with an airgun and made sure that it is safe, store it away in a locked cupboard, and store the magazine and ammunition in a separate locked box. There is, unbelievably, no legal requirement to store an airgun in this way. You could lawfully leave it propped up against a wall with the pellets on a shelf next to it. But from a perspective of moral responsibility, such behaviour would be more than woeful. An airgun can be considered safely stored only when it is locked away. In an environment where there are children, an airgun that is not locked away will sooner or later attract their attention, which makes for a potentially lethal incident. Ex-army ammunition boxes are an excellent way to store pellets and magazines; they are just the right size and can be locked.

Never leave an airgun unattended, not even for a second, loaded or unloaded. Your gun is your responsibility so it must be under your supervision at all times.

Remember that there are no justifiable reasons for contravening or ignoring safety procedures.

MAXIMUM HUMANE SHOOTING DISTANCE

You will read accounts of people shooting quarry at 36 or 41 yards. Some will even tell you how they shot a rabbit at 70 yards, but I have to question the ethical acceptability of engaging targets at such ranges.

Air rifles have a very limited level of power and are designed to work at close range, which means a maximum of 35yd (32m) with the very best weapons, 30yd (27m) for anything else. Though the full-powered legal-limit air rifle can produce enough power to deliver a killing blow to a rabbit at 40–45yd (36–40m), the level of skill required to place such a shot accurately into the tiny kill zone on a rabbit's head is phenomenal because of the trajectory a pellet would take to reach such a target. The flatter the trajectory the easier it is to pull the shot off. The greater the curve the more difficult the shot, and the curve on shots over 35yd (32m) is severe.

To find out what is involved in placing a pellet accurately at distances in excess of 35yd (32m), go and watch an airgun target shooter at work. See how much time, effort, energy and, above all skill, is required.

Shoots in excess of 35yd (32m) may well be achievable on the range where the first shot can be used as a marker but, in the field, shooting at such ranges is ethically unacceptable. Even with a good shooter, targets engaged in excess of 30yd (27m) are at very best a 50/50 shot, which is not acceptable. You should always have a 90 to 95 per cent chance of pulling off a shot, or you should not be depressing the trigger.

Personal Safety when Handling Dead Rats

The number of diseases that rats can transmit to man and other animals means that dead rats should be considered hazardous (*see* page 101). The handling of dead rats has to be done with the utmost care. Adherence to the following guidelines should prevent the contraction of any diseases.

- Never take the prone position in areas where there is rat traffic.
  In damp environments, bacteria left by the rats can thrive and you do not want to come into contact with it.
- Never handle rats with your bare hands, and do not expect cloth gloves to offer any protection.
  Rats should be handled wearing thick rubber gloves that are thoroughly washed with boiling water after every outing. When removing rubber gloves, before the first glove has completely come off the hand, remove the second glove. This way you can avoid touching the finger end of the gloves with your bare hands.
- Have a designated place where you can leave dead rats, so that the farmer or owner of the property can dispose of the rats the following day, preferably by burning.
- When working in areas of heavy rat infestations it is a good idea to seal the ends of your trouser legs – quite a number of rat catchers who did not exercise this precaution have experienced a rat up their trouser leg.

Always use rubber gloves, never cloth, to handle dead rats.

You can see from this rat that they keep their coats in excellent condition; but no matter how clean a rat looks it always poses a potential threat to human health.

CHAPTER FIVE

Ammunition

A shooter's rig is made up of three things: gun, scope, and ammunition. The pellet is the actual weapon, the gun is merely the deliverer. You could spend a fortune on a really good gun, but place in its barrel poor-quality ammunition, and you will end up with inaccurate and unreliable results.

On the other hand, you could purchase a run-of-the-mill gun, and place in its barrel the very best pellet money can buy and end up with very acceptable results. The point I am trying to make is that ammunition is not an afterthought: any old pellet will not do. You could cope with a mediocre gun and a bargain basement scope, but you will never get anywhere with poor-quality ammunition.

ENERGY RELEASE

When a projectile strikes its target, the amount of energy it releases at the point of impact is dependent on the surface area of the pellet head, and the weight of the pellet. Imagine, if you will, a block of butter that is 30cm (1ft) tall. If you strike the block from above with a knitting needle, you will make a small hole because the surface area of the needle is very small. It does not matter how hard you thrust the needle you will always make a small hole. If you get sufficient velocity behind your stab then the needle would probably go straight through the butter from top to bottom.

If we now take a hammer and strike the butter, we will inflict a serious amount of damage as the hammer has a much larger surface area; but it will mean that no matter how hard we strike the butter, we will not get the hammer to penetrate from top to bottom. The needle does not release its energy at the point of impact as it is a light, high-velocity weapon that retains its energy upon impact. This is why it travels further than the hammer and causes less damage. The hammer is a heavy, low-velocity weapon that releases its energy at the point of impact.

If we now take these findings and relate them to pellets, we see that a heavy pellet with a broad head will inflict massive tissue damage with heavy bleeding, causing sudden and very severe shock. A lighter pellet with a narrow head will penetrate deeply, doing very little damage on its way.

THE PARTS OF A PELLET

Head
This is self-explanatory: it is the front end of the pellet, the part that strikes the quarry first. It is also the part that enters the barrel first. One of its functions is to ensure that the pellet is located centrally in the barrel. There are a number of different head shapes for different functions.

Dome Head
This is quite simply a dome-shaped head. The dome head is the classic hunting pellet, providing an aerodynamic shape and a large surface

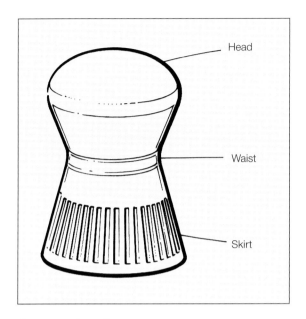

Anatomy of a pellet.

area, which at the point of impact releases its energy causing severe damage. The dome head is also very stable and accurate over long distances. This is the pellet you would choose for long-range rabbit hunting or for all-round use.

Pointed Head
This pellet has a very pointed head, which gives an amazing level of penetration – quite often far in excess of what is needed. The small surface area at the tip of the point means that it does not release its energy at the impact site, thus it does not do as much damage as the dome head. Pellets in flight from gun to

target lose energy with every yard travelled; the pointed head loses more energy for every yard covered than does the dome head. So the pointed head has less strike power.

Personally I would not bother with pointed pellets as they over-penetrate and don't pack enough punch for my taste.

Wad Cutter
This is a flat-headed pellet which was designed for use by target shooters. The idea was that the shape of the head would cut a beautifully rounded, clear hole in the target, whereas other pellets tend leave more of a tear.

The wad cutter has the broadest head of all, so it can deliver a very heavy blow indeed for an air rifle. The problem with this is that it has a very broad front which means that it slows down very rapidly, losing a lot of energy with every yard travelled. (After travelling just over 20yd/18m it will have lost almost half its energy.) This pellet can therefore be used only at short range, definitely not exceeding 25yd (23m). Within this range the wad cutter is extremely accurate and delivers a devastating level of knock-down power. Its applications are for the shooting of feral pigeons inside farm buildings and for shooting rats.

The wad cutter is a very light pellet, which means that only the .22 calibre is suitable for hunting. The .177 is a bit too light for the task. One big advantage of the wad cutter for those working at close range in enclosed spaces is that it does not over-penetrate. This pellet will stay well and truly inside the rat or pigeon.

Hollowpoint
This pellet has a dished head with the front having a concave dip in the middle. The hollowpoint is used in the same fashion as the wad cutter and is a great favourite amongst professional pest controllers.

Pellet Waist
The waist is the area directly behind the head where the pellet narrows before fanning out into the skirt.

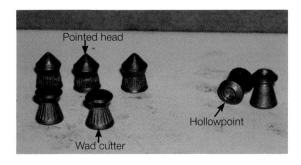

A selection of hunting pellets.

Pellet Skirt

The skirt is the fanned out area at the back of the pellet. Its job is to form a nice, tight air seal in the barrel. This forces the pulse of air to propel the pellet down the barrel, rather than escape down the sides of the pellet. The skirt is designed to expand slightly when the pulse of air strikes it, so that the seal becomes really tight. If the skirt is not perfectly cylindrical it cannot form a seal, the air will therefore escape down the side of the pellet, consequently the air will have a reduced energy level.

PELLET METAL

Lead

Most pellets are made from lead: a heavy, bluish grey metal that is very malleable. Lead is used, firstly, because it provides sufficient weight and, secondly, because it is ductile (very easily formed).

When the pellet speeds down the barrel, the skirt forms a tight seal but the seal has to give to the contours of the barrel. In other words the barrel has to be able to form the shape of the pellet as it moves down it. In order to do this the pellet must be made of a fairly soft material, because air rifle barrels are made from a fairly soft steel that can be easily damaged. If the pellet were made from a firm, unyielding metal it would literally scrape away the barrel as it propelled along; and it wouldn't take long for such pellets to completely ruin the barrel.

However, lead is a very nasty metal. In America tins of pellets, like packets of cigarettes, say that the handling of lead could cause cancer. We all know that lead can cause poisoning, which is why lead waterpipes have been universally replaced with plastic. We also see from children who stick lead toys (which are now banned) into their mouths, that a very small amount of lead ingested into the system can cause a problem. So lead may be well suited to the task, but it is not the healthiest of materials. I feed feral pigeons to my ferrets and have, in the past, had ferrets go down with lead poisoning. I mitigate against this problem now by digging out the pellet before the pigeons are fed to them, but this just goes to show how dangerous lead can be.

Napier Power Pellets

If an all-lead pellet is your preferred option, then you will be hard pressed to find a better one than Napier's Power Pellets. These come in two head types: the dome head and the wad cutter. Both these pellets are manufactured to the highest possible standards, meaning that there is a great deal of uniformity from pellet to pellet, ensuring consistency from shot to shot.

The dome head is a long-range hunting pellet with a phenomenal degree of accuracy, making it one of the most precise pellets on the market. I utilize this pellet for those very long-range shots. My usual maximum range is 30yd (27m), but sometimes a slightly longer shot is achievable (32–34yd/29–31m) if the conditions are right and you have a good gun and sufficient skill. For such shots you also need very reliable, accurate ammunition: the Napier Power Pellet with the domed head is my choice for this. It puts together a tremendously tight grouping even at 35yd (32m).

I favour the dome head over the pointed head for long-distance work because the former is better suited to flight, retaining more energy as it travels through the air. I always have about twenty of these pellets in my pellet kit when out hunting rabbits.

I put a young shooter onto these pellets who was having a real problem with accuracy, even having difficulty achieving an 3in (8cm) grouping. Once onto the Power Pellet the problem vanished and his accuracy improved dramatically, allowing him to achieve consistent 1in (25mm) groupings.

The Napier Power Pellet with the wad cutter head, is essentially a target pellet that is exceptionally accurate but only at short ranges of 10–15yd (9–13m). It is definitely not a pellet for long-range rabbit shooting. At close range it is hard to match for accuracy: its head, shape, weight, and velocity all combine to make this a really hard-hitting weapon for hammering down feral pigeons and rats.

Non-Lead Pellets

Prometheus Pellets

There is one company that offers an alternative to lead pellets. Pax Guns, based in London, produces a range of lead-free airgun ammunition under the brand name Prometheus Pellets. They are advertised in the following way: 'Dirty toxic pellets that contaminate your hands and pollute the environment are a thing of the past.' Prometheus pellets are an environmentally friendly product and have won a prestigious industry award, presented to those who manufacture in an environmentally sensitive manner. Prometheus pellets are, to my knowledge, the only pellets to have won such an accolade.

Prometheus use a non-lead alloy to produce their pellets: a mixture of non-lead metals. The mixture is not specified. This may be because they don't want competitors to know what their pellet is made of; just like good cooks do not share their recipes, pellet manufacturers do not share their secrets. The Prometheus pellet can be considered a clean pellet in that it will not contaminate your hands and it contains no toxins.

The fact that these pellets are environmentally friendly should, in itself, interest the airgun shooter. A pest controller could

The Prometheus non-lead airgun bullet.

be using anywhere between 2,000 and 10,000 pellets a year – that's an awful lot of lead to be handling and throwing about in the environment. If the pest controller had an 85 per cent success rate, he would miss anywhere between 300 and 1,500 shots, all that lead being left in the environment. What then is the impact of all the missed shots? Could wild birds, for example, pick up pellets mistaking them for seed? There has been no study on this subject so I am simply surmising. It's interesting to note that wildfowlers have had to give up using lead shot because they were poisoning wildfowl; fishermen are having to think again because their lead weights are killing swans. If you are using lead you need to be thinking about the consequences.

So, the Prometheus pellets are a clean, environmentally friendly form of ammunition. But do they work as a killing weapon? The first thing you need to know about them, is that they are not as malleable as lead so they cannot be formed by the gun's barrel in the same way that a barrel can form a lead pellet. If you put a Prometheus pellet that is too big in your gun's barrel it will, when fired, scrape away the barrel's rifling. The metal of the pellet would be too strong for the soft metal of the barrel. Pax Guns negate this problem by providing a host of material on their website explaining which pellet fits which gun. A gun barrel in .22 could have a bore of 5.54mm or 5.56mm, a barrel in .177, a bore of 4.46mm or 4.5mm. When using non-lead alloy pellets, you need a pellet that matches up exactly to the diameter of the bore. The website provides the information that allows you to do this.

The Prometheus pellet is shaped much more like a bullet than a pellet, with a very substantial dome head that gives a large surface area. This causes the pellet in .22 to dissipate a great deal of energy upon impact. But in .177 these pellets have such phenomenal velocity that they do not release much energy on impact but use it to continue travelling, giving a massive amount of penetration – in many cases more than you want. For example, I set up a tin can at 30yd

(27m) and filled it with sand; the can had a circumference of 12cm (5in) so the sand was 12cm (5in) in depth. That is a formidable obstacle for a pellet to penetrate, and yet 85 per cent of the Prometheus pellets in .177 went straight through it. The pellets exited the back of the can, with no discernible deformity to their shape whatsoever. You would only want to use these pellets at long-range; I would never use them in a confined space such as a farm building, as the amount of ricochet would be enormous.

Prometheus produces a hollowpoint pellet in .22 which is more suited to close-range work. The weight and shape of the pellet ensure that it releases its energy at the point of impact, making this a more specialized pest controller's pellet for close-range work against rats and feral pigeons. For rabbits I think the .22 dome-head Prometheus is the best option. It's a weapon more than capable of killing: it strikes hard and does serious damage to animal tissue, causing sudden fatal injures.

These pellets do not seem to have caught on as well as they should have. In the UK, shooters tend to be very traditional in their choice of ammunition, but if you give these pellets a go I think you might be very impressed by their knock-down power and accuracy.

The Prometheus can put together a tidy grouping of 25mm (1in), and I'm just a competent shot; a really good shot could do even better. I now use only Prometheus in .22 for my rabbit shooting, principally because they are a clean, environmentally friendly product and, wherever possible, I like to adopt the green approach.

Predator Premium Hunting Pellets

This rather unusual hunting pellet is manufactured for Target Sports of Bolton, a specialist airgun shop. The Predator is not entirely a lead-free pellet, but it is relatively enviromentally friendly – though not in the same green league as the Prometheus.

The Predator has a pointed head, which is made from polymer (plastic). This lightweight pellet tip has a really sharp point, a bit like

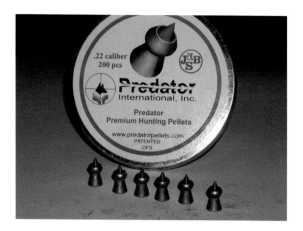

The Predator pellet with its red pointed head.

a javelin, which gives it an amazing level of penetration.

Unlike most pointed-head pellets though, the Premium does not over-penetrate. This is because the point is set into a hollow head which is broader than the base of the point, giving the main body of the pellet a substantial mass that causes the energy to release fractionally after the point of impact. So what you have is: a point to penetrate, then mass to slow the pellet down and release the energy. The pellet therefore releases its energy inside the target animal, delivering a sledgehammer-like blow, causing a devastating amount of shock, tissue damage and blood loss. It is a killing weapon of well-conceived design.

I will quite often opt to shoot a pigeon in the chest. A pellet placed within the region of the heart and the lungs will kill instantly; but it must first penetrate the breastbone. This is a tough piece of bone covered by dense muscle, vastly different from the relatively soft bone of a rabbit's skull, so it takes a bit of penetrating. The Predator is just the pellet for the job. The polymer point pierces the breastbone like a missile, then the hollow head causes the pellet to release its energy in the pigeon's chest cavity, causing the feral pigeon to drop to the ground like a falling stone. This is my pellet of choice for mid-range feral pigeon shooting between 15yd (13m) and 25yd (23m).

QUALITY

As a hunter you need to know what makes a good pellet. To do this you must first understand a small amount about the physical forces a projectile faces in flight. There are a number of physical forces that affect the flight of a pellet. The two I want to highlight are: the disturbance generated at the nose of the pellet as it pushes through the air, and the drag caused by the parted air passing into the area behind the pellet.

In order to maintain stable, forward movement in the face of these disruptive physical forces, the pellet must contain sufficient weight, have a very aerodynamic shape and be as smooth as a baby's bottom.

If the pellet is misshapen, has rough edges or it is aerodynamically unsound, it will not gain a stable flight pattern. The lack of uniformity in its shape will mean that the turbulence caused by forward movement will not be distributed evenly over the pellet's surface. This creates the kind of effect you get when trying to steer a car that has suffered a sudden puncture: controlling it is very difficult – if not impossible – because the pressures in the two tyres are dramatically unequal.

A rough or misshapen pellet, created as the result of poor design or poor manufacturing, cannot maintain a true course. They will be so unpredictable in their flight pattern that it is impossible to calculate with any certainty where they will strike. Highly professional manufacturing, with good equipment and serious quality control, is the only way to ensure that pellets are uniform and smooth.

Each and every pellet in a tin has to be the same weight and shape. Tiny variations in either will create a level of inconsistency, which will make a good grouping impossible to achieve as all the different pellets will have different trajectories.

It is vital to select top-quality pellets for your gun. They may cost a bit more but they are an essential part of successful hunting, without which failure is the only outcome.

Identifying Quality Pellets

This is actually quite a simple matter. Open up the tin of pellets and take one out. Does it feel rough and look misshapen? If so it is not top quality. Now look at the skirt of the pellet: cheap pellets tend to have a thin skirt whereas top-quality pellets have a thicker skirt; this forms a better air seal as it travels down the barrel.

Take the lid from the tin of pellets and turn it upside down. Place the pellet in the lid, now roll it from side to side. A quality pellet will roll true in a straight line from one side of the lid to the other; a poor-quality pellet will veer.

Lastly, empty the tin of pellets very carefully into a suitable container and examine the bottom of the tin. If there is lead dust or fragments of pellets, you know that the pellets are of poor quality; rust also indicates poor quality.

Quality pellets tend to come in quality packaging; that doesn't always mean a metal tin. Some pellets come in cardboard boxes so the pellets, as they rattle around which they all do, will not be damaged or misshapen by contact with the box. Contact with a metal tin can cause damage.

THE RIGHT PELLET FOR THE JOB

Many shooters go out with only one kind of pellet in their pocket, but this in effect gives them only one kind of weapon. If you take a mixture of pellets you have a variety of options. For example, when I am pigeon shooting with a .22 rifle, the Predator would be my mid-range option. A wad cutter from Napier would be my short-range option for shots in the 10–15yd (9m–13m) area. For the long-range shots at 30yd (27m), which would have to be head shots, I would use the Prometheus.

By carrying a range of pellets in this way I am able to utilize their specific qualities to meet specific situations.

Different pellets have different trajectories, so it may be necessary to alter the zero on your scope when alternating from one pellet to another, but this is no great difficulty. Range work will give you the scope setting for each pellet, so you'll just have to change settings from pellet to pellet. The ability to adjust your weapon in this way is one of the things that makes for an accomplished hunter.

ADJUSTING A SCOPE FOR MULTI-PELLET USE

Once a scope has been zeroed a lot of shooters are afraid to adjust it, fearing that it will spoil their accuracy. That is not the case at all, scopes are designed to be adjustable, so adjust them.

All you have to do if you want to take a range of pellets into the field with you is zero your rifle in with the most commonly used of your pellets at a distance of 30yd (27m); using the centre cross of a multi-aim point reticle. Once that is achieved get a pen and pad at the ready, load your long-range pellet option, and zero it in at 35yd (32m).

Use the first aim point below the centre cross, counting and recording exactly how many clicks you make to the windage and elevation turrets to correlate the scope with this pellet's trajectory. Using your record of the alterations made, apply sufficient clicks in reverse to bring the scope back into zero for the 30yd (27m) range.

With your most commonly used pellet, fire a set of about five shots, just to check that you have your calculations right. Next, take your mid-range pellet and zero it in at 20yd (18m) using the aim point above the centre cross. Again, count the number of clicks required and record that information. Once more, reverse your alterations and check that the 2 30yd (7m) zero is still accurate.

Write down clearly, in bold lettering, the number of clicks required to be applied to the windage and elevation turrets for the 35yd (32m) range to be zeroed in. Underneath, write the same information for the 25yd (23m) range. Take this piece of paper and tape it to the stock of your rifle with clear waterproof tape.

You now have easily at hand the information required for you to alternate from one pellet type to another as the situation dictates. This is the kind of approach taken by military snipers, and it gives you a tremendous amount of flexibility.

I think one of the best scopes for accommodating the shooters who wish to use a range of ammunition in the field is the new Airmax from Deben. The elevation turret is of the open design – it does not have a cap covering it. Caps have to be removed before adjustments can be made but with the Airmax that is not necessary; the weatherproof dialling knob has no covering and can be adjusted straight away. The windage turret has a cap, but there really should be no need to adjust this as the variations in the pellet's trajectory should be in the elevation plane windage, only being affected if there is a significant difference in the weight of the pellets used.

ASSESSING PELLETS FOR USE

When opening a new tin of pellets, you will need to pop to your range and send ten or so shots into a target. Pellets may vary from batch to batch so when a new box of pellets is opened, they may not be identical in every respect to the previous tin you were using; they may have a slightly different trajectory.

Shoot a few of them at a target to see if that is the case, and make any necessary adjustments to the scope. From this it should be obvious that you should not be opening fresh tins of ammunition in the field: you should take with you more than sufficient ammunition that has been checked.

Preparation is the name of the game when it comes to hunting. Some shooters cannot understand why they have such inconsistent results in the field. Often it relates to poor preparation. There used to be a saying in the military, 'Planning and preparation prevent poor performance.' You need to be taking ammunition into the field that you have checked beforehand. A sniper will go through each bullet checking for uniformity and weight.

Even with good pellets, you come across a few with dented skirts or chipped heads, making their flight unpredictable; such pellets should be discarded. All the pellets you are taking should also be clean and corrosion free. (Corrosion on lead takes the form of oxidation and appears in patches of white.)

PELLET CARE AND STORAGE

Pellet Oil

The Power Pellets from Napier are prelubricated with Napier's own brand of pellet oil. An oiled pellet is more accurate than a non-oiled pellet – up to 50 per cent more accurate. Napier's pellet oil can be purchased in a small bottle to be added to any pellet that you choose. The bottle is very small but it only takes a few drops of the oil to coat around 200 pellets. Do not get the idea, as some do, that the more oil you apply the better things will get. Far from it. Less is definitely more in this case. Use too much oil and you will cause dieseling (smoking from the barrel) and your accuracy will go to pot. Add just a few drops of Napier pellet lubricator and the pellets are transformed, becoming up to 50 per cent more accurate.

Napier's pre-lubricated high-quality pellets.

The pellet lubricant increases accuracy as well as velocity. If you take two identical pellets, lubricate one and leave the other dry, the lubricated one will have more power. This increase in power is achieved because the oil forms a chemical film around the skirt of the pellet, enabling it to form a much better and more airtight seal with the barrel. Thus, more of the pulse of air released for propulsion is kept behind the pellet. The more air kept behind the pellet, the greater the propulsive force.

The lubricated pellet also achieves greater velocity because it travels easily down the barrel; lubricated objects move more quickly than dry ones as there is less resistance. Whatever pellet you choose to use, it will perform better if you lubricate it. As a hunter, power and accuracy are key elements to your success so pellet lubrication is, quite frankly, essential.

To apply Napier pellet lube, tip 200 or so pellets into a small, clean freezer bag; apply two to three drops of lube (perhaps four drops if you are lubricating some .25 pellets). Move the pellets around gently (lead can be very easily dented so don't shake them about madly or you'll ruin them). Do not leave freshly lubricated pellets lying around for weeks upon end as the oil dries out over a period of time and the effect is lessened. It is best to do a small batch of pellets a day or two before you go hunting, then use them up over the next few weeks.

Storage

Pellets should be stored in a clean, dry container for transport into the field. I use a small fishing-tackle box, which is lined with foam and divided into several compartments. The foam padding prevents the pellets rattling as well as from being dented or scratched. It fits easily into the pocket and allows me to carry a selection of pellets. A larger fishing-tackle box in my rucksack carries the back-up supply.

CHAPTER SIX

Know Your Quarry

I could in this chapter write a few hundred words on each of the quarry species that it is legal to shoot with an air rifle; but all that would give you is a basic introduction to each of the species, which is of little practical use. To hunt successfully you need to know a lot about the behaviour and habitats of your quarry, as well as a little about their anatomy.

So I shall concentrate on what I consider to be the three main quarry species: the rabbit, the rat, and pigeon (wood and feral). (Bear in mind that legal quarry varies from one country to the next, so do ensure that you know the law that affects you before undertaking pursuit of a particular species.)

THE RABBIT

This is the magnificent quarry species that has fed this country through two world wars. Though today it is not a national favourite, it was once considered by royalty to be among the finest meats in the world, which is why monarchs of the past spent vast sums establishing well protected colonies of these small creatures to ensure that they had plenty for the table. Today, the rabbit's population is a shadow of its former self, the present population being about 20 per cent of what it was back in the war years. The drop in population is thanks to some fools who decided, in 1953, to control rabbit numbers by means of introducing myxomatosis, an insidious disease that almost took from this nation one of its most valuable unrealized assets.

There were other ways the rabbit numbers could have been reduced – more expensive ways, but ways that could have made use of all

The ghillie suit is the perfect way to completely hide yourself when ambushing rabbits.

that rabbit meat rather than riddling it with disease. Thankfully, the rabbit has come back from the point of extinction. Some rabbits now seem to posses an immunity to myxomatosis, and it must be hoped this will one day be the case with every single rabbit.

Today, rabbit numbers vary enormously across the UK: areas such as the Shetlands seem to be experiencing a mini epidemic; others don't seem to have more than a handful. Some areas, where the rabbit is scarce, have been over-hunted by short-sighted individuals; when this happens the rabbit population can take five to ten years to recover.

Over-hunting is a sin, the sin of greed, and anybody who practises it should have their right to hunt removed, and would do if we lived in one of the great parks of America. Another reason why some areas are rabbit-free is disease; not just mixie but something called VHD (viral haemorrhagic disease), which seems to have brought about fairly heavy losses in some places.

The rabbit is a survivor, and even though it has been dreadfully abused by government policy it will recover. Australia shows us why: a man named Thomas Austin imported 24 rabbits to populate his estate for shooting. They took to Australia like ducks to water, and in just six years those 24 rabbits grew into such a population that Austin had 20,000 shot on his estate. They had spread from his estate to Queensland some 650km (400 miles) away. At present, Australia has a rabbit epidemic.

Signs of Habitation

Up here on the north-east coast of Scotland, where I am located, there is an old farm dump known as the quarry. It is a huge hole in the ground full of rubble and old timber, covering about two to three acres. On one side of the quarry there is a huge rabbit warren with around 50 holes; everyone who sees it says to me that it must be full of rabbits, but there isn't a single rabbit in the entire warren.

To prove this to one person who would not believe me, I sent in a pair of ferrets who searched the warren from top to bottom and

ABOVE AND BELOW: *The ghillie suit in closer detail.*

found nothing. The point of all this is quite simple: rabbit burrows do not equal rabbits. The countryside is littered with abandoned burrows – some warrens dating back centuries, some that have not been inhabited since the release of myxomatosis. Given that the rabbit population today is about 20 per cent of what is was back in 1953, it is easy to see why a large number of warrens are now derelict.

As a shooter you need to know exactly where the rabbits live upon your ground and where they go to eat. The best way to take rabbits is to shoot them when they are emerging from the burrow to go foraging, or when they return after feeding.

You need to learn how to read rabbit. Unless they are being pursued, rabbits always use the same paths to travel to and from the burrow – they even like to place their feet in the same spot every time they travel the path. The tracks rabbits make are called runs and the keen observer can soon find them.

If you look at a park, playing field or even a lawn, you can see where people have walked the same route on a regular basis as the grass is worn down or completely worn away. The track left by a rabbit is just the same, only much narrower – about 10cm (4in) wide.

If you walk around a field of grass that is not too tall (such as you find in autumn/winter fields of hay or silage that have been cut) and look across the field you will see runs if rabbits are present. If you follow these runs they will lead you in one direction to the burrow, and in the other direction to the feeding grounds. The runs may well branch off in places; at some points they may look like a rabbit version of spaghetti junction. When a run comes to a fence, you will see a clear hole through the vegetation that emerges onto a run in the next field.

I have read all manner of comments in all manner of books about how far away a rabbit will feed from the burrow. Some suggest it is only a matter of feet, but I have observed rabbits feeding up to 800m (half a mile) from their burrows (they are able to cover that distance in 30 seconds to a minute).

Runs are not the only indicator of rabbits nor are they entirely definitive. In winter, if a run should fall into disuse it will not rapidly disappear as it would in the summer because the vegetation is dormant. Runs could fall into disuse because the rabbits have died through predation or disease, or they move because of burrow flooding. Runs by themselves in the

Rabbits shot by an air rifle provide excellent meat as the air rifle, unlike the shotgun, does not pepper the carcass with shot.

winter are not conclusive; you need further evidence.

You need to be looking for droppings. Droppings appear as the natural result of digestion but they are also used to mark boundaries. The buck rabbit will make a small scratching in the ground then deposit a number of droppings, which acts as a warning to other bucks not to trespass.

If you find such scratches in the earth, you know there is a buck rabbit active in the area and he will most likely have a colony of eight or so does. There may also be in the colony of subordinate bucks, which in turn will have their does, creating a very clear hierarchy.

Rabbits produce prodigious numbers of droppings, which are actually referred to as pellets. If a burrow is in use, there should be a nearby latrine that the rabbits use communally. On feeding grounds – areas of grass crops or other herbage that have been nibbled low – there will be droppings scattered about in a random fashion, deposited as the rabbits feed. If you see runs and droppings you are beginning to build a picture of where the rabbits are living and feeding.

Look now for bits of fur, snagged on barbed wire perhaps or floating around on the feeding grounds where two bucks may have come to blows. You may also find fur and remains left behind from a fox kill, which is a good sign as foxes always know where the best hunting is to be found.

A final aid to locating rabbits is a method used by animals, but neglected by man: the sense of smell. I can smell rabbits, especially bucks, because I have trained my sense of smell to recognize the odour and when I get to within several feet of a buck I can pick up his scent.

Once you have a good idea where the rabbits are located, visit the ground in the early morning or at dusk with a pair of binoculars and observe the burrows from some distance to see what the population consists of.

At this time you should also be looking for ambush locations: sites within range of the burrow that will give you a good vantage point whilst offering some cover. Observe how the rabbits disperse to their feeding grounds and try to identify ambush locations that are not crossed by the dispersing rabbits.

It's well worth making sketches of the burrows with notations as to the wind direction and the direction of the sunrise. If you

Getting George, my pony, to carry the rabbits home for me.

intend to shoot at dawn, you will want the sun behind you. Also make a note of the rabbit dispersal and ambush sites and anything else you think relevant.

Rabbits are not stupid and only the shooter who takes the trouble to study his quarry very carefully will be really successful.

Rabbit Response to Potential Threat

The rabbit has highly developed senses. Exceptional hearing evidenced by the large ears, good eyesight and keen sense of smell. The first indicator of your presence to reach a rabbit will be your scent, which is why you should not use scented toiletries, aftershaves or perfumes on the day you go hunting.

The rabbit has underneath its nose, covered by soft flaps, two sensory pads which trap scent allowing the rabbit to fully analyse it. The rabbit gleans as much information from a drop of scent as you would from a page of text. Suffice to say that a rabbit will smell you coming long before you arrive, which is why a lot of hunters try to approach their quarry downwind: they want to walk into the wind so that it carries their scent away from the rabbit. I am not so convinced this is essential as rabbits when picking up scent do not seem to panic; they digest it, consider it, and generally do not flee. When rabbits perceive a threatening scent they become very alert but do not start running. I have managed to get within 3m (10ft) of rabbits with my scent being blown straight at their powerful little nostrils. A rabbit trusts in its legs, the speed to deliver him from danger, so he does not flee until he feels you are too close for him to run away.

I have stood in the open at 20yd (6m) watching rabbits that can clearly see and smell me, yet they did not flee, though they were extremely on edge like a coiled spring. One sudden movement on my part and they were off like rockets. Movement is the trigger that sets rabbits into flight – not scent, not sight – which is why, to successfully shoot rabbits, your movements must be invisible.

Rabbit Statistics

Colour
Head and back: Grey-brown
Belly: Grey-white
Neck: Orange-brown
Variations: Black and white
Upper surface of tail: Black-brown
Ear tips: Brown

Size
Head and body: *c.* 40cm (15in)
Ears: 6–7cm (2–3in)
Average weight: 1.5–2kg (3.3–4.5lb)

Breeding
Season: Usually January to August. If the weather is mild and conditions favourable rabbits may breed all year round
Gestation period: 30 days
Number of young: average 5

Lifespan
1–3 years

Habitat
Almost anywhere there is grass and cover

Diet
Herbage of various kinds, including grass and farm crops

When to Go After Rabbits

Rabbits come into the open for a number of reasons, the main one being to feed. Most of their time is spent underground or in deep cover away from the eyes of potential predators. The rabbit is therefore at its most vulnerable when it is feeding. As a potential predator you need to know when a rabbit goes out to feed, as this is the optimum time for success.

According to Bob Smithson, one of the country's most respected rabbit catchers, rabbits feed twice during the night: just after dusk (dark during the winter months) and after midnight. So the best time to take rabbits is at dusk and after midnight. In the right areas rabbits can also be taken during daylight hours. Such areas are where burrows are close to heavy cover: in woodlands or under large stretches of gorse bushes. Where heavy cover like this exists, rabbits will come out during the day, especially when the sun is shining brightly, playing and feeding just feet away from the burrow. Rabbits busying themselves just feet away from the burrow can be taken successfully by the hunter who is skilled in fieldcraft and who is suitably clothed (*see* Chapter Seven).

THE RAT

I have read many books that describe the rat as a filthy creature. This is an erroneous statement that could not be further from the truth. The rat is in fact, a scrupulously clean creature that pays close attention to the grooming of its coat. When you get around to shooting rats, take a good look at their coats and you will discover that they are sleek and pristine, even though they often live in filthy places. A dirty rat is a sick rat.

Having said this, the rat carries many diseases that can have an effect on the health of man and his domestic livestock. Some of the diseases that rats can transmit cause sickness; others can cause death. The urine of most rats carries spirochaete bacteria called *Leptospira*. These bacteria can survive in damp environments, just lying around waiting to infect someone. This is why water that rats have had

When ratting at night you will need a small lamp mounted on your rifle – such as this Atom from Deben.

access to is so dangerous; and why many wells in times past gave sickness and death to those that drank from them.

If you are shooting in damp environments where rats are present, be very aware that leptospirosis can result if the bacteria enters the skin through cuts or abrasions; so gloves are the order of the day in rat-infested environments. Once the bacteria have entered your system, they multiply rapidly in the bloodstream then invade the liver causing jaundice, before settling in the kidneys where in severe cases they cause death by kidney failure.

The XL Tactical in .25 is the perfect ratting rifle.

Threats to Health

Human Health
Leptospirosis (Weil's disease)
Murine typhus
Salmonella
Numerous viruses
Numerous parasites such as fleas

Animal Health
Leptospirosis (Weil's disease)
Brucellosis
Salmonella
Aujeszky's disease
(Rats are also believed to spread foot-and-mouth)

The rat is a small, fast-moving quarry so it makes a very challenging target for the airgunner.

Many rat catchers during the Victorian era died as a result of this disease, then known as 'rat catcher's yellow'. Many farm workers and coalmen also used to contract the disease, but it is much less common today owing to the heavy decline in rat numbers and the improved (relatively rat-free) living conditions of human beings. However, it does seem likely that it may become more prevalent in the future. Many councils appear to be reducing their pest control activities, which can only lead to an increase in rat numbers. If we combine this with the warmer winters and the evolution of a super rat, immune to poison, we could well be looking at a boom in the rat population in the not too distant future.

You may think that it is a bit of an irrelevance bringing up the disease factor in such detail, but anyone going after rats needs to be fully aware of the dangers these small creatures pose to human health. I have seen far too many people handle rats in a cavalier fashion that puts their health at serious risk.

Not only do rats spread dangerous diseases, they can cause substantial losses to grain stores. In a world where grain is becoming so sought after, supply in the not too distant

Sometimes rats can be taken during the day, but usually only where large infestations occur.

future is highly unlikely to meet demand, so losses will become an even greater problem. It is likely that there will be opportunities for those able to clear rats to make a bit of money. I personally will never clear rats for free. Rat shooting is potentially dangerous, very time-consuming, and requires a lot of equipment and even more skill.

Rats also make themselves unpopular by causing damage to property, which can be catastrophic and very costly. They have been known to undermine concrete foundations. It sounds impossible I know, but when 500 rats make their home under a building their constant burrowing activities, creating mile upon mile of tunnel, can literally bring a house down.

Rats are also responsible for causing fires by gnawing through electrical wires and gas mains; and when they turn their attention to water pipes a house can soon be flooded.

The Character and Abilities of the Rat

Rats are the most resourceful and intelligent quarry that you, as an airgun hunter, will face. They can reason, jump, swim and climb. They apparently have pretty poor eyesight but they make up for it with the most acute hearing and amazing sense of smell. They are extremely social, living in colonies that can be extremely large indeed.

I remember seeing a colony of 500 to 600 rats near a grain store; they were like ants, so close together you couldn't have dropped a blade of grass between two of them; the whole colony constantly on the move, each grabbing its bit of grain and scoffing it down. Sights like this send a shiver down the spine of even the most hardened rat catchers. If you are one of those people who fears rats, you will never become a rat shooter as you will need to be within 25–30yd (23–27m) of such colonies, and that is closer than most people have the stomach for.

Rats are, for the most part, nocturnal. They use the cover of darkness to try to evade their many enemies: cats, foxes, stoats, owls,

ABOVE AND BELOW: *Using a small terrier like this in conjunction with the airgun can have a very rapid effect on a rat population.*

dogs, and man. Rats have a compulsive urge to burrow, especially in soil, but I have seen them burrow into stone walls, rock piles, straw stacks, and compost heaps; in all of these locations they soon build up an extensive burrow.

They like to live near water as they are big drinkers. In the country they can often be

found along the bottom of hedgerows or along ditches adjoining farmland, where they can find ample food during the warmer months, but when the harvest is over they move into the farmyards to look for their food, making winter the busiest time for the country pest controller.

In urban areas, rats will live anywhere that offers them some source of food and water: factories, houses, cold stores and sewers. All of which have been colonized and so the urban airgunner could find himself called to a back garden, or a large industrial complex.

Signs of Rat Habitation

Runs

Like rabbits, rats make runs (paths that are regularly used when the rat is travelling between burrow and food.) They are narrower than rabbit runs and are often visible in the vegetation around farm buildings, factories or in back gardens. You will need to find these runs and follow them from the burrow to the rats' feeding ground, which is where you will set up your ambush.

Smears

Rats like to move with their bodies in contact with the ground, which results in smears being left on surfaces such as concrete or wood. These dark, greasy smears are usually found up against a wall, as rats do not like to move across open ground. A rat will always move along a wall, which is quite a clever tactic as it means that it only has to watch one side for potential predators.

Droppings

Rat droppings are sausage shaped with pointed ends, and are about 18mm long. When fresh they have a moist shiny look; older droppings are hard and dry. Rat droppings will vary in colour according to the diet, but they are usually dark. When large and small droppings appear together, it is evidence of a breeding colony and urgent action is required to prevent their spread.

Gnawing

Rats gnaw to keep their teeth in shape, to get at things they want, and also because they seem to enjoy it. The signs of gnawing can be seen on wooden doors, pallets, and pipes; basically anything that can be gnawed. A rat can, during the course of a single evening, gnaw straight through a perfectly sound, thick, wooden door.

Tracks

Rat tracks (foot prints) can often be found in mud, dust or any soft surface. The four claws of the front foot, and five claws of the hind foot are very prominently marked. Along with the foot prints you may well find a void in the dust, dirt, or mud, that looks like a piece of cable has been dragged through it; this is of course the track left by the tail.

Rat Statistics

Colour
Head and back: Grey-brown
Belly: Paler than back, usually white or cream

Size
Head and body: 20–25cm (8–10in) (females usually smaller than males)
Weight: 300g (10½oz)

Breeding
Season: Summer and autumn, but all year round where conditions are favourable
Gestation: 21 to 24 days
Litter size: 7 to 10
Sexual maturity: 2 to 3 months

Lifespan
9 months to 2 years

Habitat
Towns, cities and farmland. Anywhere that can offer food and water source

Diet
Eats almost anything, but has a liking for cereals

When examining ground for signs of rat infestation, always be aware that the environment is potentially hazardous, so wear gloves and be careful not to cut yourself. If you should cut yourself then seek medical advice as soon as possible, explain to the doctor that you were in a rat-infested environment at the time of the injury.

PIGEON

The feral pigeon, which inhabits so many city centres and farms, is a descendant of the rock dove, which nests in sea caves. As with the swallow, the rock dove soon discovered that buildings make much warmer homes than caves, where they are also much nearer to a food source. So the rock dove swapped its caves and made its new home within the boundaries of human habitation.

Man (being ever resourceful in a time when food supplies, especially in winter, were fairly scarce) soon realized that he could harvest a bountiful meat crop from the feral pigeon, which bred all the year round under favourable conditions. Special dovecotes were built to enable the rock doves to flourish.

Feral Pigeon Statistics

Plumage Colour
Most feral pigeons have a blue-grey colouring with white on the rump and underside of the wings; but there is massive colour variation, including pure white, buff and pure black

Size
Length: 33cm (13½in)

Breeding
Nest: Nests, found on ledges, are formed from twigs and grass
Eggs: One or two per clutch with an average of five clutches per year. The egg is white, 31mm long and incubation lasts for 17 days. The egg is incubated by both sexes
Young: The young are fed by both parents and can fly at four to five weeks

Habitat
Towns, cities and farmland. Agricultural and industrial buildings are favourite haunts

Diet
Seeds; scraps thrown away by humans

A fair bag of pigeons taken with a very basic spring gun.

Pigeons often fall into hard-to-get-at places.

Returning home with a nice string of feral pigeons.

The utmost care must be taken clambering around on the roof of farm buildings.

Retrieving my quarry.

When shooting feral pigeons you will often be shooting into dark corners of farm buildings.

About 150 years ago, the agricultural revolution brought about an improvement in the food supply and the dovecotes fell into disuse. This caused the valued, semi-domestic rock dove to become the despised pest, the feral pigeon.

Pigeons are not as wary as the other quarry dealt with in this chapter. They do not hide away so infestation of feral pigeons is self-evident in the presence of hundreds of birds. The challenge that pigeons present to the shooter lies primarily in the fact that they never stay still – and they don't 'freeze' as rabbits do. They also have a canny streak – they seem to know what a gun is for.

Reasons for Control

Feral pigeons are unwelcome because they devour large quantities of grain, and deposit copious amounts of corrosive droppings that can spoil grain and damage valuable machinery. Having droppings on the fresh paintwork of a new tractor is far from desirable. Feral pigeons, which some people also refer to as flying rats, are also vectors for the spread of disease.

Home-grown vegetables and farm-shot feral pigeons can make an excellent meal.

CHAPTER SEVEN

Fieldcraft and Field Equipment

Fieldcraft is the ability to move about in the countryside in such a way that you can mask or hide your presence from the eager senses of your quarry. It is also about understanding your quarry (*see* Chapter 4) and knowing how to approach it. Good fieldcraft requires an acute awareness of sound, movement, camouflage (concealment), other wildlife, and odours.

SOUND

- Sound is caused by movement (foot-fall on leaves, dry twigs, rocky ground, and so on), equipment rattling, or talking. What might appear to you to be a tiny whisper is, to the ears of your quarry, more like raised voices would be to us.
- Sound carries further and, unlike movement, is most perceptible during the hours of darkness.

MOVEMENT

- Movement is most perceptible during the hours of daylight.
- The eyes of rabbits and pigeons are equipped to react to the tiniest of movements.
- Quick and jerky movements will be detected more easily than slow, deliberate ones.

When in a hidden position for ambushing quarry, remain as still as possible, remember that movement attracts attention. Stop, look, and listen often so that you are aware of your surroundings.

The hunter in the open stands out clearly, but the hunter who moves in the shadows is far more difficult to see. Shadows exist under most conditions, day and night. On open ground use ditches, stone walls, and hedging to give you some concealment. Never move across the middle of a field, always round the edge even though it is a longer route. Avoid skylining: a figure on the skyline can be seen from many miles away. Walking along the brow of a hill for example would put you on the skyline; walking the base of the hill will keep you in cover and under shadow.

Do not move aimlessly: always have a clearly planned route across your shooting ground. Always move slowly, placing each foot with the greatest of care aware of what is underfoot; remember that the slightest sound can be heard some considerable distance away by your quarry. When observing or moving into a shooting position, stay low, as a low silhouette is more difficult to pick out than a standing one.

Crawling

There are four types of crawl: low crawl, medium crawl, high crawl, and hand and knee crawl.

Low Crawl
This crawl offers you a very low profile, it can be used to make final adjustments to your

The low crawl. These crawling techniques are possible only if your rifle is fitted with a sling; these can be purchased along with the necessary fixings from Garlands.

The medium crawl. On all crawls it is essential to keep the face down so that it is not seen by your quarry.

shooting position when you are close to your quarry.

Lie flat on the ground with your head turned to one side. Your arms should be stretched out straight in front of you above your head, and your legs should be almost together in a straight line to the rear. The gun is held by the sling, parallel to the body.

Movement is achieved by pushing slowly and evenly with the toes, whilst pulling forward with the fingers. The intention is to move up to no more than 10cm (4in) at a time.

Medium Crawl

This crawl gives a slightly higher profile than the low crawl and is intended to be used to take you into your shooting position.

Lie flat on the ground with your head to one side, arms raised above your head, and your legs about shoulder width apart. The weapon is held by the front sling swivel, and is draped across the forearm.

Movement is achieved by raising one leg so that it is bent at the knee, then pushing with the toes of the bent leg while pulling forward with the arms. This will take you 30–40cm (12–16in) at a time.

High Crawl

This crawl is designed for covering larger distances such as open ground when moving from one area of cover to another.

Lie on the floor, the upper body supported by the elbows and the lower body supported on the knees. Cradle the weapon across the forearms, with the scope between the chin and the chest.

Movement is achieved by moving the elbow and knee on one side forward, then moving the elbow and knee on the opposite side forward.

Hand and Knee Crawl

This is used to reduce the height of the profile in areas where there is some medium-height undergrowth to shield the hunter.

High crawl. Note how effective the Jack Pyke camouflage is, even against this snowy background.

Hand and knee crawl.

Get down on your hands and knees, only one hand goes on the ground; the other is used to cradle the weapon, tucking the scope under the armpit.

Movement is achieved by moving one knee forward, then the other; then the single supporting hand is moved forward.

CONCEALMENT

There are two basic kinds of concealment: hiding and blending.

Hiding
Hiding is completely concealing your body from observation, by lying behind an object or thick vegetation, or by concealing yourself in some form of hide.

Blending
Blending is accomplished by skilfully matching your personal camouflage with your surroundings, to the point where the hunter becomes indiscernible. This is best achieved by wearing a ghillie suit.

The term ghillie suit originated in the Highlands of Scotland during the 1800s, when Scottish gamekeepers made for themselves camouflage suits to catch poachers. The ghillie suits of today are specially-made camouflage uniforms with a net base that is covered with irregular patterns of garnish.

My ghillie suit is manufactured by Jack Pyke, an English company whose parent company manufactures products for the British Army. My ghillie suit is a magnificent piece of camouflage: when it is on, my outline disappears and I simply become a bush – a huge great bush that can merge into any rural setting whether that be woodland or pasture. The Jack Pyke ghillie suit is made up of a jacket, a hood, and leggings.

There is not a camouflage pattern in all the world that can compete with a ghillie suit, as

The complete Jack Pyke ghillie suit.

no matter how good camouflage clothing is it just does not break up the outline so completely as does the ghillie suit. You can see for yourself from the photos that it is a complete transformation from human to vegetation. They're not cheap, but they are without doubt worth every penny and will enable you to get unbelievably close to your quarry.

One little tip when it comes to ghillie suits: cut a little hole in the veil in front of your shooting eye so that you get a clear view through the scope.

Camouflage

The purpose of camouflage is quite obvious: it is to make you merge seamlessly with your surroundings so that you become invisible to the quarry.

Improper camouflage is anything that contrasts with your environment, making you stand out. It might include the following:

- Anything that shines, such as a highly polished rifle.
- Anything that has clean, unbroken outlines: any clothing that does not break up the shape of the human outline.

Camouflage Clothing
Is camouflage essential? Strictly speaking no it is not: you can hunt successfully without. What it does do, however, is make your task easier and, by doing so, probably leads to a bigger bag.

To be effective, camouflage clothing must replicate the flora and fauna of the British countryside. If we look at some of the rabbit's predators, the fox and the stoat for example, we see animals that have an exceptionally effective camouflaging coat. It may not be a mixture of greens and browns, but the fur coats of both animals blend magnificently with the natural environment. The fox has a fairly bright red colouring, and the stoat has his russet colouring bordering on red, and yet when either of these creatures decides to hide itself it can become invisible, seamlessly blending into their surroundings. If the fox and the stoat are camouflaged we should follow their example.

It surprises me that some enterprising clothing manufacturer has not produced a camouflage pattern based on the colouring of the fox or the stoat. The closest thing is a russet-coloured tweed which, it has to be said, provides excellent concealment. If the floral type of camouflage does not appeal to you, then why not wear tweed which is exceptionally effective and hard-wearing to boot.

Unfortunately, nearly all the camouflage patterns on the market are designed for the American environment; and though there are many similarities between the flora and fauna of America and the UK, there are also many differences. So it is fairly valid to ask the question, are the American patterns the

Notice the subtle difference between camouflage designed for the American countryside (above) and Jack Pyke camouflage designed for the British countryside (below).

deciduous trees are bare so you want a camouflage that combines green leaf with russet colours as does the Jack Pyke pattern.

Camouflage, especially for the airgun hunter who works at such close quarters, has to be made of a material that is silent. It must not make a noise when the wearer moves. Jack Pyke uses cotton to the same standard as that used in the manufacture of British army combat jackets. So you can trust their products to be totally silent.

When you examine clothing in your local gun shop, give it a shake to see if zips or buttons clink; ruffle up a sleeve to see if it makes any noise.

Camouflage clothing has to be very generously cut to allow the shooter to adopt all manner of positions; tight clothing and shooting just do not go together. The Jack Pyke clothing that I use is very roomy, but to prevent winds getting underneath the jacket and up the trouser legs, draw cords have been sewn into the ankles and the waist of the jacket. The draw cords at the ankle are also very useful for stopping small branches and stinging nettles popping up the trouser leg.

How Much Camouflage Clothing Do You Need?

If you intend to hunt on a regular basis, say twice a week both summer and winter, then you will need the following set of clothing:

- camouflage jacket (one summer weight, one winter weight)
- 2 pairs of camouflage trousers
- 2 pairs of fingerless gloves
- 1 camouflage neck warmer
- 1 camouflage hat
- 1 fleece jacket
- 2 army-style belts
- 1 pair of lightweight stalking boots
- 1 pair of wellington boots
- 1 ghillie suit
- 1 large holdall
- 1 rucksack
- 1 small game bag.

best choice for the UK hunter? Personally, I think we are better off selecting a camouflage that was specifically designed for the UK. A company called Jack Pyke, the same company that makes my ghillie suit, does a range of camouflage clothing with a pattern that is based on the ancient woodlands of Britain.

As you can see from the photo above, it is much darker than the American patterns. The pattern is a mixture of winter and summer foliage, so it can be used all the year round. Owing to the dark sand base on which the pattern is laid, it also blends nicely with grassland areas, making it effective in a variety of locations.

You want to be careful with some camouflage patterns because they are based too heavily on green leaf. As we all know, in the winter the

At the time of writing, some camouflage clothing manufacturers charge £180–200 for a coat, and around £80 for a pair of trousers. At these kinds of prices it would cost over £1,500 to put together this list of clothing, which is, quite frankly, beyond the means of most people. The above list from Jack Pyke, however, would cost less than £500 – still quite a lot but the ghillie suit accounts for £120.

WILDLIFE

You must be aware of other wildlife in order to avoid disturbing it. Disturbance usually means spooking birds – a pheasant in the rough or a crow in a tree whose sudden flight will advertise your presence to every quarry species in the vicinity. Always be on the alert for wildlife of any kind because if they spot you before you spot them they could give your location away.

ODOUR

Odours that can be detected by your quarry include the following:

- soaps and lotions
- perfume
- smoking
- insect repellents.

KEEPING WARM AND PROTECTED

Carrying out ambush techniques during the winter requires seriously warm clothing. Lying out in temperatures close to freezing, made worse by the wind chill, can bring the inadequately attired shooter dangerously close to hypothermia. Quite aside from the health risk, cold has a detrimental effect upon muscular coordination and judgement, which will very adversely affect your marksmanship.

Dressing correctly is all about layering, beginning with a thermal layer – long-johns and long-sleeved vest. Over the vest you

The Jack Pyke hunting jacket and trousers – a very warm winter combination.

want a Norwegian shirt, which is designed for Arctic conditions. The Norwegian shirt has a roll-up collar that zips all the way to the chin (zip it right up as the speed at which heat is lost around the neck is second to speed of loss from the head). Over the long-johns you need camouflage trousers that have a lining to prevent wind penetration. Over the Norwegian shirt wear a fleece, I favour the Jack Pyke fleece because it is not only warm but waterproof. Over the fleece goes a well-padded winter jacket. The Jack Pyke field jacket has a thermal liner that makes for an exceptionally warm garment; the outer of the coat is a very robust cotton designed to protect the inner coat from damage. This jacket is very much along the lines of the M65 jacket as worn by the American GIs during World War II; it gained a reputation as an extremely tough, functional garment.

As an airgun hunter there will be a lot of crawling over rough terrain to get into position. This is obviously very abrasive on clothing, and many modern man-made fabrics will not tolerate such treatment, but cotton seems impervious to such abuse. This is why the military favour it and why Jack Pyke stick with it. There are some very tough man-made fabrics. Cordura, for example, is lightweight and almost indestructible; the only problem is that it cost a fortune. I have an excellent cordura suit in green, from a company called Schoffel; it is truly a magnificent suit of clothing, specifically designed for the UK environment, but obviously not everyone can justify such expense.

The next thing required to keep you warm in winter is a hat. I must admit that I loathe hats but you need to cover your head, and in some weather conditions even your face, in order to maintain warmth during the winter as the head accounts for the largest loss of body heat. If you are a hat wearer then go for something with a warm fake fur lining with fold-down earflaps, or you could go for a fleece or wool balaclava. My brother, an avid hat wearer, reckons that wool with some kind of canvas lining is best. Whatever your taste, the head needs to be covered.

Tactical Gloves

Now to the hands. The airgun hunter's hands get bashed and bruised, stung by nettles and pricked by thorns, not to mention the fact that they get cold. The hands need serious protection, but there is of course a problem: you need to be able to use your hands for loading and for trigger manipulation.

It has taken me many years of searching but at last I have found a glove that is perfect for airgun hunting. It is a tactical fingerless glove made from leather. It's the type of glove worn by SWAT teams and the like.

It has raised padded sections across the front to protect the back of the hand from knocks and abrasions. You could literally slam your hand into a concrete pillar and you will not sustain any serious damage, such is the level of padding in the raised protection areas. The palm of the glove is suede, which makes for an exceptionally tenacious grip in wet and dry conditions. The fingerless design means that you can handle pellets with ease, as well

On snowy days like this a hat such as the Jack Pyke trapper hat is essential.

Tactical gloves, like those used by SWAT teams.

as being able to operate the safety catch and manipulate the trigger. These gloves are manufactured by a company called Viper, which makes tactical vests and equipment for SWAT teams and other agencies. I would have to say that these gloves have become an indispensable piece of equipment.

FOOTWEAR

For your feet, you're going to need a range of footwear. On and around farmyards, especially during the winter, you will need a good pair of wellington boots.

The most important thing as regards wellington boots is to get a pair made from natural rubber. Man-made versions will make your feet sweat profusely, creating an unhealthy (and uncomfortable) environment for the foot. For the winter, wellies need some form of lining: a thick layer of neoprene is quite effective; fake fur linings are also very good.

The legendary Irish setter boot from America.

For winter hunting in the field, especially when ambush techniques are employed, you will require a heavily insulated leather boot with a waterproof lining. These can be very expensive indeed. I wear a pair of Irish setters (style No. 859), an American boot designed for use in the Rocky Mountains. This is an absolutely unbeatable boot – I have never found one to equal it in quality or performance – but they are extremely expensive.

For stalking, you need extremely lightweight footwear that allows you to feel the ground beneath your feet. There is another Irish setter (style No. 869), whose design is based on the Indian moccasin concept, giving you the ability to read the ground you are walking on.

If you can afford only one pair of boots, set aside the wellies and the stalking boots and go for a midweight, waterproof, leather boot – the type of boot worn by the police and the army. Inside your boots wear a double layer of socks. You need a breathable base layer over which you wear a heavier-weight woollen sock, preferably merino wool. I wear Rohan socks. They are not cheap but they are good; if you skimp in the sock area, going for a cheap and cheerful type, you will soon pay the price with feet like blocks of ice.

FIELD ACCESSORIES

Lamps
If you intend to go shooting at night (lamping), or inside buildings, you will need a scope-mounted lamp. The lamp that I use is designed for professionals, its power source being a 6V 3Ah battery that fits into a pouch for attachment to a sturdy belt. For lamping rats, 3Ah is about the maximum power rating that you would want.

My lamp is manufactured by Deben and is called the Atom Pro. It is an extremely lightweight lamp that simply clips onto the scope's body tube. The Atom emits a very bright light, which is concentrated into a narrow beam that will illuminate the target but not bleed out into the surroundings. This is vital when operating in areas where stock are present:

you need to light up your target without throwing light all over the stock that may get spooked by the light.

The Atom has a red filter that clips onto the front of the light's housing. This allows for a very soft light, which is ideal for close-quarters shooting as it gives sufficient light for the scope to operate in. The Atom has a control switch that fastens to the stock so that it is easy to find and operate. Though the light comes with materials to attach it to the stock, I prefer to tape my switch down using insulating tape; I also tape down the wires so that nothing can get snagged in the dark.

In addition to the scope-mounted lamp you will need an observation light, such as a low-powered torch.

Belt

The airgun hunter needs a belt on which to carry his knife and the battery packs for his night lamp. Forget the thin leather belts and go for an army-style webbing belt. These are darn near indestructible and will take an incredible amount of weight. The thickness of the belt means that whatever item you carry upon it, the weight is spread over a broader area than would be the case with an ordinary leather belt, making the load more comfortable to carry. The belt that I wear is made from ballistic nylon and comes from the Viper company.

A military style belt.

Bags and Rucksacks

For a day's shooting you will need the following:

- pellets
- ghillie suit
- pump to refill the air bottle should it run low
- tripod
- drink and snack
- binoculars
- map
- first-aid kit
- torch
- boots (and a plastic bag to put them in when they are muddy)
- rope.
- sand sock (used to provide support for springers)

In addition you should have a blanket in your car. I use a holdall from the Jack Pyke range which swallows all the gear with the greatest of ease; it also has eight large external zipped compartments so I can arrange my gear in such a way that it is easily found and accessed. It is not practical to carry this holdall out into the field, so I leave it in the car. For carrying your gear into the field, you will need a smaller bag or rucksack in which to carry the following:

- pellets
- drink and snack
- first-aid kit
- binoculars
- rope
- the quarry you kill
- matches or, preferably, windproof lighter.

I am very lucky in having a small pony to carry my load on ground that is near to my home, but since the pony cannot fit in the car I need to take bags when I am working further away.

On small shoots, where I expect to take just a couple of rabbits, I will take a Jack Pyke dog bag, which is basically a small game bag in which I carry my supplies. Then I will leg the rabbits, rope them together, and carry them

Jack Pyke holdall (left) and rucksack (right).

slung over my shoulder. On bigger shoots where I expect to cover much more ground and take five to ten rabbits, I will take a rucksack.

The rucksack carries my few pieces of equipment in the side pockets, leaving the main compartment free for carrying rabbits or pigeons, whichever the case may be. It is essential that the inside of the rucksack is washable as it will get covered in blood.

I have two rucksacks, a 25-litre Jack Pyke and a larger canvas Roe sack, from a company called Garlands. Both are excellent for swallowing up the day's rabbits. The smaller 25-litre one will hold five to six, the bigger Roe sack around ten – about as much weight as most people can manage.

When stalking quarry, take the rucksack off and place it to one side before you begin the stalk; then come back to collect it when you have bagged your quarry.

Knives

One of the hunter's most important pieces of equipment next to his gun is his knife. I have built up a collection of very good knives over the years, but I shall only place three before you.

The first thing that you want to know about knives is that you need quality; a cheap knife is a useless piece of equipment that will rapidly shed its edge. In order to purchase a quality knife you need to go to a quality manufacturer. I am an advocate of British manufacturing, but when it comes to knives the Americans and Scandinavians have the edge.

Buck are my favourite knife manufacturers, an American company that has a world reputation for excellence. The company was founded over 100 years ago by Hoyt Buck, who made the first lifetime knife. A Buck knife properly cared for (which does not mean pampered), will outlive you.

I like to carry a very big knife, but with the knife laws of today and people's sensibilities, I carry such a knife only when I am in remote rural locations where I will not encounter a single soul, except perhaps the farmer who owns the land.

My favourite Buck knife – the Omni.

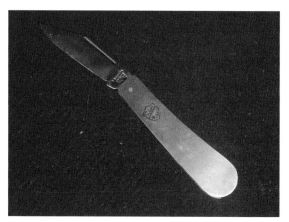

A Rodgers pocket knife.

My favourite large knife by a mile is Buck's Omni Hunter (photo). It has a 10cm (4in) broad blade, and a curved handle that sits superbly in the hand. I am so fond of this knife because it is what I call a 'full-blooded' field knife: it can tackle any reasonable task without flinching – whether it be cutting rope or making wooden pegs. The Omni is also a first-class skinning knife, especially when the knife is required to work between the skin and flesh, dividing the two with clean even strokes, in order to make pelts.

Though the blade is big and broad it is extremely thin, thanks to Edge 2× technology. This process, exclusive to Buck, allows them to make blades that are thin and flat, yet incredibly strong. The blade is made from a steel that goes through a state of the art heat treatment, producing a razor-sharp, corrosion-resistant blade that is easy to sharpen.

They say that Buck knives start sharper and stay sharper for longer. That is certainly true in my experience. I have spent a fortune on knives that were razor sharp when I bought them, but soon lost their edge and could not be re-sharpened no matter how hard I tried. With a Buck knife, a few rubs with a quality Arkansas honing stone has the edge restored to razor sharpness.

The handle is made from thermoplastic and has a grip pattern over the surface, meaning you can hold on to the knife with ease, even when your hands are soaked in water, blood, or mud.

The sheath is made out of ballistic nylon and it has a drainhole in the bottom, which is an excellent idea. Wet knifes when returned to the sheath have a small amount of run-off, which can pool in the bottom of the sheath. If there is no drainhole, the damp environment at the bottom of the sheath becomes a breeding ground for bacteria, making it unhygienic.

When hunting in slightly more populated areas – a golf course or recreational woodlands for example – I leave the Omni at home and take a folding knife with a lock blade. On such occasions I carry a Swedish-made knife, which is specifically designed for Scandinavian fishermen, so it has an incredible grip and a razor-sharp point that is ideal for gutting and legging rabbits. It can fit unobtrusively into a small pouch on my belt underneath a coat or fleece.

When shooting in heavily populated areas, such as on the edge of towns or in and around industrial buildings, the only knife I carry is a non-locking penknife, less than 7.5cm (3in) in length. Such a knife is totally legal (the other two cannot legally be carried in public places); nevertheless you still have to prove you have a just reason for the carrying of a knife if challenged by the police.

The penknife that I carry comes from a British company, Rodgers, who have been manufacturing penknives for a staggering 300 years. The Rodgers pocket knives have a stainless steel blade that is robust, easily sharpened and that holds its edge nicely. I use their design No. S90S, which has a clip point blade ideal for legging and gutting rabbits and a metal handle that is riveted together. Though small and light this knife, which incidentally is very inexpensive, can easily skin a rabbit and will last a very long time if properly maintained.

I am never without my Rodgers pocket knife: of all my knives it is the most often used.

SAFETY

Whenever you set out on a hunting trip, leave with a trustworthy person a card containing the following information:

- the date
- the time you will be setting out on your trip
- your shooting location (given as a map reference and place name)
- the registration number of your vehicle
- the time you are expecting to return
- contact details for next of kin.

The person holding the card can then contact the authorities if you do not return at the expected time. When you do return from your trip, do not forget to inform the person holding the card or you may be responsible for a false alarm.

First-Aid Kit

You should never go into the country without a first-aid kit, the means of lighting a fire, a blanket, water, torch, and some food in your car. Injuries are thankfully rare, but when they do occur you may well be in an isolated location, hours away from medical assistance; it could be winter time and it could be during the night. You should therefore be equipped to deal with emergencies from a broken limb to heavy bleeding. A company called Web Tex, suppliers to the British Army, do a comprehensive first-aid kit used by the army, which you should carry on your belt or in your bag every time you go into the countryside.

Along with the first-aid kit, I carry a small bar of chocolate and a small vial of honey.

When I cut myself on some rusty old bit of metal, or on anything else that could contaminate the bloodstream, I apply honey to the wound. Honey contains substances that prevent the build-up of infection. This is scientifically proven, which is why honey is now used in hospitals on serious wounds that conventional treatments cannot deal with.

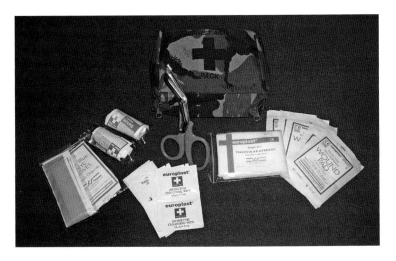

A first-aid kit is essential for everyone venturing into the countryside.

Don't forget that there is not much point having first-aid and survival equipment if you do not know how to use them, so read a few books on first aid and survival.

Fluids

When out hunting you should carry with you a bottle of fluid. Hunting requires quite a bit of walking, sometimes mile upon mile over rough terrain, which leads to a loss of body fluids. If this is not corrected it will eventually lead to dehydration. Wind, sun and cold also all have the ability to dehydrate the human body, so you need to be taking fluids at regular intervals – a few mouthfuls every 15 minutes or so.

Obviously you cannot lug a bottle around with you, but Jack Pyke do a lightweight aluminium flask that is ideal for the purpose. I carry an isotonic drink in my flask. It is a liquid that is rapidly absorbed into the bloodstream. To make this isotonic fluid I take half a carton of orange, apple, or grape juice and add to it four or five teaspoons of brown caster sugar; it dissolves rapidly. I then take half to three quarters of a teaspoon of salt, stir it up, and you have a very effective isotonic drink.

QUARRY-SPECIFIC FIELD-CRAFT AND TECHNIQUE

Rabbits

Ambush

The best way to take a bag of rabbits during the day is to wear heavy camouflage, preferably a ghillie suit.

Make your way to burrows that you have studied previously, where you know that the rabbits feel confident enough to come out during daylight hours. Before you arrive at the burrow you should have clearly established in your mind the location you are going to take, which should afford you a good view of the burrow but shields you from view. You will need a route to your chosen location that hides you from the eagle-eyes of the rabbits.

When in position do not rush your shot. Consider the scene and select your target.

Don't go for the rabbit that is biggest but the rabbit that presents the best option for a clean kill. That will be a rabbit that is side-on to you with a clear view of its head. Your chosen target should be settled so that you do not have to rush the shot. If no rabbit presents such a shot do not pick the best of a bad lot and take a chance; just wait and watch, like a cunning fox would do until things change and the shot presents itself.

When you have taken your shot, if you have killed cleanly do not break cover (if you have injured the rabbit then you must break cover and dispatch your quarry quickly and humanely). The rabbits may bolt below ground in response to your shot; if they don't, take another shot, but don't rush your target selection.

If the rabbits go below ground, hold your position for another 30 minutes or so as they may well re-emerge.

Stalking

Stalking begins with walking your ground, going to areas that you hope will be frequented by feeding rabbits. During daytime, these will again be areas close to heavy cover: along the edge of a woodland where it borders a meadow. Your objective here is not to take up an ambush position, but to stalk within range of the identified target, take the shot and move on to seek out more targets.

You want to begin your stalk from about 100yd (90m) away, using a small pair of binoculars to identify the target and to scan the ground for the route that provides the best cover.

If you want to learn how to stalk rabbits you need to watch the fox at work. I'm sure most of you will have seen some wildlife documentary that has followed the fox; and you will have seen how when foxes are stalking a rabbit, every single movement is in exaggerated slow motion, each foot being placed with the greatest care.

You will also have noticed that the fox does not take the most direct line from his position to the rabbit, but will go considerably out of his way to take a line that has the most of the available cover. The slow, deliberate movements and the indirect line to the rabbit, mean that the fox will have to invest quite some time into the stalk; it is not a five-minute undertaking. For every three stalks the fox engages in, it is probable that only one will be successful.

In order to stalk rabbits, you're going to need time, patience, controlled movements, and a little bit of luck. When a fox is moving in on a rabbit he never takes his eyes off the prize, not for a single second. If the rabbit shows any sign of becoming nervous: the raising of the head, sitting up to listen, or if it should move, the fox freezes and drops slowly to his belly and waits patiently until it has settled.

This is one of the most important factors in any stalk: reading the mood of your quarry and halting your movement when the quarry becomes nervous. If you ignore this principle and try to force the stalk, the rabbit will cotton on to your presence and bolt.

The fox almost always ends his stalk by crawling into the strike position on his belly, I think it is well worth copying the fox, moving into your final position on your belly using the sniper's crawl.

Lastly, after all this effort do not waste it all by rushing the shot. Take a moment to compose yourself then line-up the shot in a methodical, unhurried fashion. The slow, deliberate, well-thought-out shot will always be better than a rushed one. In the Wild West, a quick draw was not as deadly as the movies make out; it was the ability to slow things down, so that you aimed straight and squeezed the trigger gently that was truly deadly.

Stalking is, without doubt, the most challenging way to take rabbits as it requires an advanced level of fieldcraft.

Lamping Rabbits

When shooting rabbits at night, I tend to get between the rabbit's feeding ground and their burrow so that any rabbit that I light up with the lamp will freeze rather than run. I will move into position without the aid of

For lamping you will need a lightweight lamp that attaches to the scope tube. These two from Deben – the Mini with a 250m beam and the Atom with a 100m beam – are both excellent for the purpose.

any light whatsoever, using fence lines to guide me as the wire can be seen even on the darkest nights.

Once in position, I scan the rabbit's feeding ground with the red filter over my lamp; any rabbit that stays still and is within range will be shot from the kneeling position. If the rabbit is too far away to be shot, I remove the filter and stalk the rabbit with the bright white light upon it.

Some rabbits just freeze when the white light hits them, others hop away. If they hop they generally go only a few feet before pausing. I keep following them with the lamp until they eventually freeze long enough to give me a chance at a shot.

A lot of shooters tend to go lamping very late at night, but I find that I see more than enough rabbits at around 7 o'clock during the dark winter months. The best nights for lamping are very dark, fairly still nights; but I have discovered that rabbits will in fact come out on most nights even if it's only for a short while.

Rats

Unlike rabbits, rats do not hang around when scent or sound pricks their senses. The instant a rat is aware of your presence it is off. Having said that, the urban rat can, in some circumstances, become quite brazen if it has become accustomed to human activity. Sewer workers come across rats that do not flee from them, which is probably because rats in that environment do not have any predators, and so have no need to flee.

Rats in the country, however, will flee the very second they sense your presence; so you will need to learn how to move your gun slowly and silently to the shoulder to take the shot.

Because the rat is so sensitive, the only really successful way to take them is to ambush them near their feeding sites. Walking around the farm or factory looking for rats will only yield the occasional kill, as most will hear you coming long before you see them.

Firstly, you need to identify the rat's foraging site – by following runs from the burrow to the foraging site, which will be littered with droppings and show signs of feeding activity.

Next, select a very well-concealed spot that gives you a clear line of sight. If no hiding place is available, make one out of straw bales, pallets, or whatever else is available. Then go away and do not visit the site for about a week, as rats are very sensitive to change and may well avoid the area for a while.

Your hiding place needs to be about 25yd (23m) away from the rat's foraging ground. You will need to take up position in your hiding spot shortly after dark. Don't wear any smelly soaps, aftershave, perfume, or other products that have an odour, even a mild one; they will betray your presence.

Your rifle will need to be equipped with a scope-mounted lamp (*see* photos on page 121). At the very close range at which you will be engaging rats, you do not want the kind of lamp that is used by fox shooters, which lights up half a field. You need a much more subtle device.

You will also need an observation light to observe your shooting ground so that you can see when the rats arrive. This needs to be a fairly low-powered torch, preferably with a red filter; I use a miner's lamp that fits on my head. You do not use your scope lamp for observing the area because powerful scope lights only offer an hour or so of light, and if you are waiting 55 minutes for the rats to appear then you won't have much light left to shoot with when they arrive.

When the Atom Pro lamp (*see* page 121) is fitted with its filter, the soft nature of the light seems to have a calming influence on the rats, unlike a bright white light which tends to send them scuttling for cover. You also do not want to be lighting up the entire area at once, illuminating every rat in range, as the light tends to put the rats on their guard. You want to be able to zone in on a small area with just a couple of rats in it, then move the beam round. The rats outside the beam should then, hopefully, just carry on about their business.

When the rats do eventually arrive, move your rifle slowly up to the shoulder and switch on your light; direct it to one side of the rats, then slowly drift the red beam onto them. If the rats get the slightest bit agitated by the light, pause the movement of the beam and start it moving again once they have all settled.

How Long Should You Hang Around
Rats could appear in a group of two or three, twenty or thirty, or a hundred or more. Where numbers are low you will probably only get the one shot and then they'll disappear. The sound of a rifle, even when it is well silenced, is enough for the sharp ears of a rat to pick up.

But where numbers are high, you will more than likely take a number of rats before they cotton on to what is happening and depart.

Some people hold their position and wait for the rats to reappear, which could be some considerable time, but I do not. I will walk around stretching my legs, hopefully picking off the odd rat here and there as I wander around, then I will take up another ambush position well away from my first site and see what that has to yield.

In places where there is a really heavy rat infestation, walking around the site for a few hours night after night could well yield some pretty big tallies – up into the hundreds.

Feral Pigeon

There is no great skill required to locate the feral pigeon. They are not like rats or rabbits, which hide their presence. A pigeon believes his safety lies in flight and in perching high above his enemies. For this reason the feral pigeon is in plain view.

Shooting feral pigeons can be extremely demanding on the marksmanship of the shooter. Firstly, they are generally above the shooter which necessitates a standing shot; the standing shot being the most challenging shot of all. (For standing shots try to use pillars or walls for support.) Then there is the fact that feral pigeons rarely stay still and, as has been noted in Chapter 6, they seem to know what a gun is all about.

For all these reasons, the pigeon shooter needs lightning-fast gun handling – not rushed but quick and controlled, which is the product of hour upon hour on the range doing rapid fire exercises. (*See* box.)

Before you pull the trigger on a pigeon, there is one essential check that you must make. For pigeon shooting you will be using a scope with a wide field of view, which will enable you to glance quickly at the pigeon's legs to see if it is wearing a ring (these are usually brightly coloured). This is very important because a ring signifies that it is a racing pigeon. It is quite common for racing pigeons to mix with ferals. Racing pigeons can be very

---

Speed Practice For Pigeon Shooting

To hone your shooting skills for pigeons, set up three or four separate targets – tin cans with a 25mm (1in) square of black tape stuck on will do nicely. Shoot them as quickly as you can whilst retaining accuracy, going straight from one can to the next. Regular practice at this will increase your speed considerably.

---

valuable but, much more important than this, they are much loved by their owners. Shooting a racing pigeon is like shooting somebody's dog, so have a care not to kill one of these trusting creatures. If you can get ridiculously close to a pigeon, always suspect it is a racer because they are, after all, used to close human contact.

Lots of buildings where feral pigeons are present have a dozen or so holes in the roof offering the pigeons an escape route, so when you come through the door the pigeons will start moving towards the exits. Try to use as much cover as possible (although there is often very little available). I wouldn't bother building a hiding place to ambush ferals, as once they have heard the first shot they will start leaving the building, and can then be gone all day.

I tend to target the birds nearest to an escape hole in the hope of causing a bottleneck; this usually allows me to bring down three to five pigeons before they escape. Sometimes, pigeons enter a sound building through a door that has to be left open during the day. When that is the case, I get permission to shut the doors so that the pigeons are trapped inside the building. I can then shoot each and every one.

I did this inside a shed used for storing cattle feed and brought down forty ferals in just over two hours. Try to carry out this kind of cull humanely. The birds realizing they are trapped will panic, so be as quiet and still as possible; every time the flock takes to the wing give them time to settle before you take the next shot.

Shooting pigeons inside a building will require a torch. The Deben Atom I mentioned (*see* page 121) is an ideal choice. As with rats you will want it fitted with a red filter, as pigeons generally spook in bright white light.

In some places the pigeons will be found outside on the rooftops. The most difficult task in such cases is getting close enough to the pigeons to deliver an effective shot. The ridge of an agricultural or industrial building may be 30–40ft (9–12m) from the ground. You only have an effective range of 33–38yd (30–35m), which means that you will have to be no further than 50ft (15m) away from the base of the building. The area around buildings rarely offers much in the way of cover, apart from the odd tractor, but the one thing that you do have in your favour is that pigeons on rooftops tend to see themselves as invincible, so you may well be able to get within range.

If your pigeons are of a more nervous nature and just won't let you get within range, taunting you by moving up and down the roof to get out of sight, then the best way to deal with them is to scare them off the rooftop by throwing pebbles or shooting in the air; you must

then hope they will land in a place where they present a more achievable target.

Judging the range from your position to the pigeon on a rooftop can be a challenge, but the illustration below should help you.

When shooting pigeons on rooftops, I find it best to take the target that is furthest from you first: the most isolated member of the group. You need to aim for the head, hoping it will simply fall back when hit causing no disturbance to the other birds. If you were to start with the bird in the middle of the group, surrounded by keen little eyes, you are much more likely to cause a disturbance. When the bird is down, move to the next most isolated target.

Shooting pigeons presents a big problem when it comes to retrieval. They don't always drop obligingly to the ground: quite often they get stuck in rafters or they fall into guttering. If you are not prepared for such eventualities, a good portion of the bag will remain unretrieved.

I deal with this problem by carrying a ladder and an extendable pole in the car, which can be utilized to get me within reach of my pigeons, but be very careful climbing onto roofs. Get

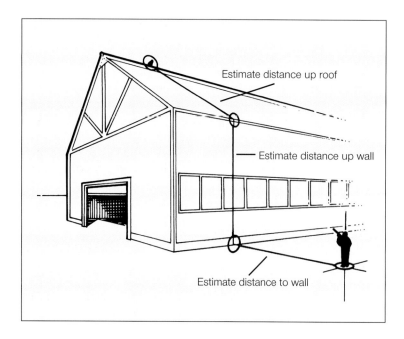

Estimate distance up roof

Estimate distance up wall

Estimate distance to wall

Judging the distance from your position to the rooftop. Add all three estimations together to give the range.

the permission of the property's owner first, who may well require some form of disclaimer in case you should fall and break your neck.

There is another way to shoot feral pigeons: scatter about five handfuls of top quality grain in some predetermined spot that suits your needs, somewhere near to good concealment from which you can shoot. Poultry corn is good but the best is pigeon mix, made for racing pigeons. You can purchase it by the kilogram from pet shops.

When you have sprinkled your pigeon mix in the desired place, retreat to your hiding place. Don't forget you need to be hidden from birds flying overhead, not just birds that have landed to feed. It shouldn't take the keen eyes of the pigeons long to spot the delight you have laid down for them.

If a number of birds come in to feed, select the target that presents the most achievable shot; you may only get the one shot before they fly off again so make it count. If the bird is killed then stay undercover and await another visit. If the bird is not killed go and dispatch it, then return to your hiding place; showing your face may have blown your cover, but give it another go before you abandon your hiding place.

Wood Pigeon

If you live in certain counties such as Cambridgeshire, where I once resided, you will see a lot of wood pigeon. Should the opportunity to hunt them come your way, take it. Wood pigeon provide good-quality meat that can be turned into some tasty dishes such as pigeon pie.

Wood pigeon shooting with an air rifle is a rather specialized activity, involving the laying of decoys. Apart from the fact that I don't do much of this kind of shooting, going into the subject of decoys could swallow up several chapters. If wood pigeon shooting takes your fancy you can learn all about the weapons, ammunition, scopes and shooting techniques from this book, then turn to a specialist publication on wood pigeon shooting – of which there are a good few. It doesn't matter that

they are written for shotgun users because all you want them for is to learn about the laying of decoys. But remember, you only have an effective range of about 35yd (32m) so don't go laying the decoys too far away from your hide.

For wood pigeon shooting you will need a long-range rifle fitted with a high magnification, long-range scope. The perfect example is the BSA Super Ten mounted with a Hawke Varmint 6–24×44. An ultra-accurate rig like this will be essential as you will be limited to headshots.

This is the only time I would suggest a .177: the flat trajectory of the .177 suits long-range shots better than any other calibre. The .177 pellet is not a very big or weighty projectile, but you only need a small projectile in the brain of a wood pigeon to kill it outright.

Wood pigeon shooting takes place from a hide and people often recommend the use of a carbine for such situations; but with the long range involved in shooting wood pigeon I think a standard rifle length is theoretically better. A long barrel should be more accurate than a short one. Don't worry that you will not be able to operate a full-length rifle inside a hide. After all, the main hunters of wood pigeon are the shotgun brigade, and shotguns most certainly do not come in carbine lengths.

The shotgun user has an advantage over the airgun user in that he can take birds in flight. The shooter with a shotgun can take a much bigger bag. On the other hand, pigeons taken by the airgunner will not be peppered from end to end with shot; therefore, the airgun user can take meat of a better quality that will be easier to prepare and better to eat.

If wood pigeon is your intended target then spend plenty of time honing your skills on the range at 35yd (32m) targets until you can constantly achieve a 1in (25mm) grouping.

HUNTING AT NIGHT (LAMPING)

Lamping obviously takes place at night, when the countryside is cloaked in blackness. For the uninitiated, it can be a dangerous place.

I live on a very tidy, five-acre smallholding; on the darkest of nights I can find my way around with the greatest of ease without a torch and without bumping into things, but that is because I live here and know every dip and rise of the ground like it was the back of my hand. If, however, you were to put me into a strange environment that I had not studied very closely, I would very quickly walk into something or trip over. You might think that this is an irrelevance, because the lamper carries a powerful torch and so can navigate the ground safely no matter where he is, but that is not the case at all. Even the very best of lamps do not illuminate like daylight, and lamps, by their very nature, create large areas of shadow.

If you visited a strange place in torchlight and then revisited the following day in daylight you would be amazed to discover how much you had missed. If you intend to lamp over a piece of ground, then you need to know that ground inside out.

I remember when I lived in Wales on a rented holding, for which I did not have the shooting rights, a lamper turned up one night who had never visited the ground before and proceeded to go lamping with a high-powered .22 bullet rifle.

What absolute folly! He did not know the ground so could not know what was in the area behind the rabbits he was shooting at. He didn't know which fields contained stock and which did not. He did not know where the

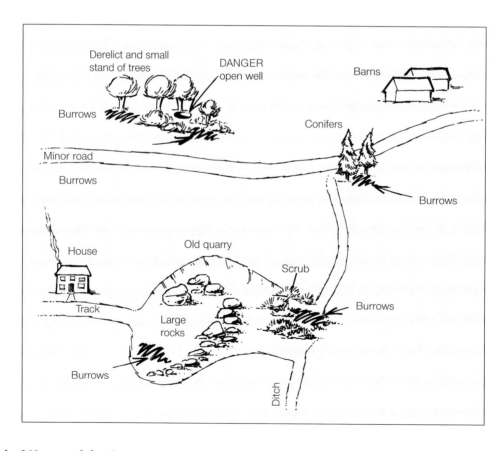

Sketch of 60 acres of shooting.

dangers lay. He was a cowboy, a chancer, and one day he could well end up injuring someone or himself.

Even on ground you are very familiar with, everything changes in torchlight, distances don't appear the same, and shadows can make familiar objects that you're accustomed to look completely different.

Negotiating ground safely at night is down to meticulous preparation. Visit the ground during the day. Walk it over and over again making detailed sketches. The first thing that you need to know is the locations of your quarry, which means identifying rabbit burrows that are in use or sites where rats are feeding. The next thing you need to make a note of are the dangers – a field containing a bull for example.

The first thing you may hear if you step into a field with an angry bull in the darkness is the sound of thundering hooves. By the time you have located the charging animal with your lamp, it may be too late to evade the giant creature's iron head; so know exactly where the bulls are located before you visit. It's not just bulls that can be a danger: cows with calves at foot can also attack. Every year a significant number of farmers are attacked by cattle, and these are professional stockmen.

If you are going shooting on a beef or dairy farm, you will need to know the location of the cattle before you visit so that you can plan a route that takes you around, rather than straight through the middle of them. If you have not visited a farm for a few weeks do not take it for granted that all the stock will be where it was the last time you visited. Stock moves around the farm periodically so check

with the farmer before you visit to make sure nothing has changed.

I once turned up on a farm without checking to see if anything had moved and came face to face with a bull known for its aggression. Fortunately I have worked with cattle in the past and was able to extricate myself very carefully, the bull following my every step snorting menacingly. Had I panicked I would have been charged down and trampled. Animals sense and smell fear and it seems to make them attack.

If you're ever faced by an angry cow or bull, keep calm, face the brute and walk backwards with slow deliberate steps. Turning your back and running is madness: unless you happen to be an Olympic sprinter, the cow is going to outrun you and, with your back turned to it, you cannot make any evasive moves.

Another danger that should be noted is water: rivers, streams, ponds and wells. A man can drown in a very small amount of water, and if you have not studied your ground very well it is possible in the dark to walk straight into a river – even if you are carrying a torch.

You should have on your sketches a note of any drops. I have been on farms that were close to the sea and had at their boundary cliffs with a sheer drop of hundreds of feet. Abandoned farm machinery, not as common as it once was, can present a real threat to health. A bit of rusting metal sticking up out of the grass may not seem deadly during the daylight, but walk into it at night with the result of torn valuable clothes and a cut leg, and you may think differently; rusting metal can lead to tetanus (lockjaw).

In short, always study your ground properly beforehand.

CHAPTER EIGHT

The Law

If you want to shoot, it is essential that you know the law as it applies to shooting and that you work responsibly within its confines.

UK AIR RIFLE USE AND OWNERSHIP

If you do not have a Firearms Certificate, you may own a rifle with a muzzle energy that does not exceed 12ft per lb. Most manufacturers do not produce guns right up to the legal limit because, depending on the kinds of ammunition and lubricant used, air rifles can fluctuate slightly in their power levels. A weapon bang on 12ft per lb might just tip beyond the legal limit, in which case you would be in possession of an illegal firearm – an offence that the courts take very seriously.

It is your responsibility to ensure that your guns stay within the legal limits; you do this by checking them with a chronograph on a regular basis.

Age
You must be 18 years of age to own an air rifle and buy airgun ammunition. A shooter aged between 14 and 18 may shoot unsupervised on land that he has been given permission to shoot on. However, you must be 18 or over to carry an air rifle in a public place, so those below 18 will need to have someone take their gun to and from the shoot for them. Shooters aged under 14 must be supervised at all times when using a gun; the person supervising must be aged at least 21.

Purchase of Air Rifles
If you are buying from a gun shop, that shop will be a registered firearms dealer. They must sell guns face to face: they cannot send them to you by mail order. When you purchase an air rifle from such a shop, your details will be entered into a register to show that the weapon is in your possession.

You may purchase an air rifle in a private sale, from a private individual who has advertised their weapon for sale in the papers, or on the internet; in these cases your details are not registered. Allowing private sales to continue unmonitored is in my view ridiculous; since the ownership of these guns is not registered, there will be a vast number of air rifles in circulation that are completely untraceable. Personally, I think that every rifle in the UK should be registered with its serial number and the person who owns it and, if that rifle is sold on, registration should be transferred accordingly.

LEGAL QUARRY

Mammals
The brown rat may be shot but not the black rat, which is protected by the law. The grey squirrel may be shot but not the red squirrel, which is also protected by the law. The rabbit

may be shot. There are a few other mammal species, but these are the main ones. To ensure that you stay well within the law you need to study the physical characteristics of the grey and red squirrel, and the brown and black rat so that you do not make any mistakes, and can identify these mammals with ease.

You do not need a game licence to shoot rabbits. It is enshrined in law that a landowner has the right to take rabbits off his own land and he can delegate his shooting rights to another; this should be done in writing. The landowner can if he wishes revoke the shooting rights at any time he chooses.

The law does not stipulate a closed season for rabbits, but I believe there is a moral case for a short closed season (between May and September).

Birds

All birds, even those considered vermin, are protected under the law and may not normally be killed or injured. Certain species may however be dispatched under certain strict conditions. These certain species include wood pigeon, feral pigeon, collared dove, rook, carrion crow, and magpie. The shooting of these species is allowed under a general licence issued by DEFRA (Department for the Environment, Food and Rural Affairs, England and Wales), and the SE (Scottish Executive).

This general licence allows the landowner to kill such species if they are causing damage to crops or stored feed, or if they are endangering the health of livestock. The landowner may authorize others to carry out the killing of these species on his behalf. Those authorized to act on the landowner's behalf should have their authorization confirmed in writing, signed by the landowner.

The terms of the licence require that the person killing the above species can demonstrate – to a court, if necessary – that the species killed at the time of being killed were in the act, or about to engage in the act, of causing damage to crops or stored feed, or posing a threat to the health of livestock.

If a couple of wood pigeons are roosting in a tree above a field of grass, they do not fall into the above category. Many birds are shot in just such a situation. However, strictly speaking this is unlawful. Similarly, many rooks, jackdaws and magpies are taken in situations were they do not present a demonstable threat.

Transportation of Weapons

When in public places the rifle must be covered up, a gun bag is used to do this (*see* photo on page 113).

It is an offence to fire an air weapon within 15m (50ft) of a road or street.

CHAPTER NINE

Maintaining Your Hunting Rifle

It is not a lot of good being able to shoot a rifle and take quarry if you do not know how to maintain a rifle. The unmaintained air rifle will, in a very short space of time, become rusty, inaccurate and unreliable. In this chapter we shall look at the following:

- how to clean and lubricate a rifle
- how to fill the air reservoir on a PCP
- how to fit a scope to a rifle
- how to use a chronograph
- how to completely strip down the XL Tactical
- how to install a tuning kit into a spring-powered weapon.

The PCP has a major weakness: there is very little in the way of maintenance that the DIY gunsmith can carry out if anything goes wrong. These guns have to go to a qualified gunsmith or back to the manufacturer. Tamper with a PCP and you could quite easily create a lethal weapon that could kill you, so leave the PCPs to the professionals.

CLEANING AND LUBRICATING A RIFLE

If a rifle is wet, wipe it down with absorbent kitchen towel and remove the stock. The stock is held to the action with one or more screws (as many as three). The BSA Ultra, for example, has a single screw on the underside of the forestock, 10cm (4in) in front of

Step 1.

Step 2.

the trigger guard. The XL Tactical has three screws, one on either side of the forestock, and one at the back of the trigger guard. Whatever arrangement you have, remove the screws and separate the stock from the action (Step 2).

Brush away all dirt with a paintbrush reserved for this particular task.

Remove the silencer and clean the barrel with a pull-through. (The best pull-through kit on the market is, in my opinion, the Napier power pull-through kit. It not only cleans but lubricates the barrel, optimizing power and accuracy.)

With the barrel as clean as a whistle, it is time to turn your attention to the outer surface of your rifle, which will rust if not correctly cared for.

The product recommended by BSA for the care of a gun's metalwork, is the Napier Field Patch. These are large cloths impregnated with 2ml of Napier gun oil that has been blended with VP90. (VP90 is a powerful corrosion inhibitor that completely protects a gun from rust and will resist fingermarks on the blueing.) The VP90 forms a self-healing skin over the entire rifle, preventing air and moisture penetration. Simply wipe the cloth over the entire surface of the gun (Step 3).

Wood, just like metal, needs nourishment. The stock requires the application of a suitable oil, and for this you want an organic rather than a mineral oil. I use Abbey stock

oil, which is a linseed oil. Pour some onto the stock, rub it in, and buff up.

With a PCP, this is the end of the cleaning process for the rifle; now all you have to do is put the stock and action back together.

Spring-powered guns require grease. Once a month on a regularly used gun (not every time you clean), apply some grease (never oil) to the main spring (Step 4). You must use moly

Step 4.

grease (moly is short for molybdenum disulphide). I use Abbey LT 2 (Step 5), a grey moly-based grease that is recognized as a superior lubricant.

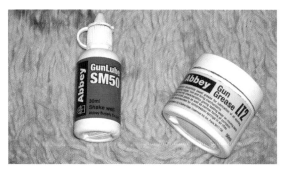

Step 5.

Turn the action upside down. You will see a slot through which the spring is clearly visible. Coat the spring with grease, using a cotton wool bud. Don't go mad – a light application is all that is required. I also apply a smear of the grease to either side of the breach jaws to ensure smooth opening and closing of

Step 3.

the barrel. A light smear over the face of the barrel latch is also advisable (Step 6).

Step 6.

Once every two months, apply a couple of drops of Abbey gun lube SM 50 to the trigger, paying particular attention to the sear (the part of the trigger that holds back the spring when the gun is cocked). I also apply a dash of the SM 50 to the safety catch which, if not regularly lubricated, soon becomes stiff.

Cleaning the Barrel with a Pull-Through Kit

Spray power airgun oil down the barrel and leave it to stand for about a minute.

Push the string-looped end of the pull-through down the muzzle end of the barrel until the loop comes out at the breech (Step 7).

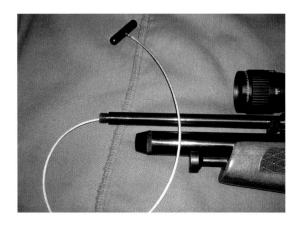

Step 7.

Take some pre-lubricated cleaning patches. (The number of patches will depend on the calibre of your weapon. Two patches for .177, three patches for .22, and four patches for .25.) Never use more than the specified number of patches.

Thread the patches through the loop. (Step 8.)

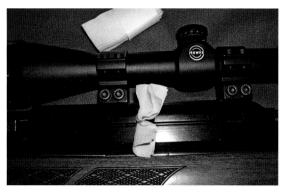

Step 8.

Pull the patches down the barrel until they come out the muzzle end. Apply constant pressure to the pull, and pull straight, not allowing the wire of the pull-through to rub against the barrel. If the wire of the pull-through rubs against the inner surface of the barrel, it can cut into the bore, causing serious damage to the crown (Step 9).

Step 9.

Take the patches out of the loop and send it back up the barrel. Reverse the outer patch so the clean side is facing up. Place the patches back in the loop and once more pull them down the barrel. Keep drawing patches down the barrel until they emerge clean. On the third time of pulling the patches through, take an inner patch and put it on the outside.

Once the patches are emerging clean, stop the process and spray a very small quantity of Napier airgun oil down the barrel. This will provide lubrication and complete protection from corrosion.

Lubricants, oil and grease do not last for ever. They dry out over a period of time as the result of exposure to the environment. The action of the moving parts of a gun relies on regular lubrication. A gun left unlubricated for as little as a month will begin to show signs of rust.

Remember that too much oil or grease is as detrimental as too little: it will attract dirt and become, in effect, a grinding paste rubbing away at the metal like emery cloth.

FILLING AN AIR RESERVOIR

The air used to fill a PCP has to be of a very high quality. The air must be clean and 'dry' before it can go into the reservoir as unclean air can cause internal blockages in the gun's air system, and moisture in the air rots the air reservoir from the inside out. PCPs cannot be filled from any old air compressor; the reservoir must be filled from a compression system that produces dive-quality air (air of the quality used by divers).

About every two years, have your charging gear (air tank, and adaptor) safety-checked by a recognized service facility; this could be your local gun shop or a dive centre.

There are several ways of filling an air reservoir. You could take your gun to the nearest gun shop and have them fill it for you, but for any serious shooter this would mean going back and forth like a yo-yo.

Preferably you could have your own air tank from which you fill up the gun. It is basically a

Step 10.

diver's bottle with a special adaptor on the top (Step 10) that allows it to be connected to an air rifle. A tank of this nature, dependent on its size, will fill up a rifle between 18 and 40 times. You can have such an air tank filled at your local gun shop or at a diving centre.

The other way to charge up your PCP is to use a hand-operated stirrup pump (*see* Step 11 overleaf). I use this method because it is the only filling system that offers complete independence; with a tank you have to have access to a filling facility; the hand-operated compression pump makes do with the air around it. There are a number of such pumps on the market but there is only one that I would recommend: the Hill's hand-operated compression pump. (It is also the only pump recommended by BSA.)

A pump takes air from the environment and, as the air is drawn through the pump, it is cleaned and dried. Most hand-operated compression pumps have a series of filters to do this job, whereas the Hill's hand-operated pump has a more effective system: a chamber filled with an organic compound that the air must pass through. This organic compound draws moisture from the air. No other

Step 11.

Step 12.

hand-operated compression pump has such a system. This is why the Hill's pump is considered to be the market leader.

Now to the actual charging of the gun. There are two distinct types of PCP: those with an integral air reservoir and those with a removable bottle. We shall deal with the integral reservoir first, using the BSA Ultra as our example.

Charging the Integral Air Reservoir
Check that the rifle is unloaded and that the safety catch is on. Cock the weapon by depressing the end plunger.

Remove the end cap, located below the silencer, to reveal the air inlet (Step 12).

Your adaptor, which comes with the rifle, should be attached to the hose of your chosen charging system. Examine the small rubber O rings around the top of the adaptor. If these are damaged replace them as you will not create an air seal with damaged O rings.

Apply a small amount of Molycote 111 grease to the O rings (this can be purchased from BSA), then insert the probe into the air inlet (Step 13). **Do not use any other lubricants on the probe: incorrect lubricants can cause explosions whilst charging**.

Step 13.

If using a Hill's hand compression pump, close the airtap (Step 14) and begin pumping. If the air reservoir is low you will need to do quite a bit of pumping. As you get close to filling the reservoir you will feel strong resistance. Watch the gauge (Step 15) on the pump: when it reaches 200 bar for .22 and 232 bar for .177, stop pumping as the rifle is full. Putting more than the specified amount of air in the rifle will not create more power: it will in fact damage the weapon and could be dangerous.

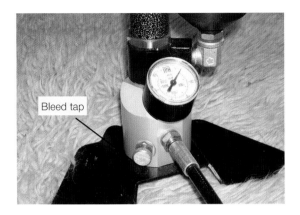

Steps 14 and 15.

Once the required charge has been achieved, unscrew the airtap, which will release the pressure on the line, allowing you to withdraw the probe safely.

Replace the end cap and de-cock the weapon (do this by depressing the plunger and hold it down, then release the safety catch and pull the trigger). You will now feel pressure on the plunger, which you should release slowly.

If you are charging the reservoir from an air tank after attaching it to the rifle, open the main airtap on the tank slowly to allow air into the rifle's reservoir (if you fill the reservoir too quickly you will overheat it, making the air within it volatile). Close the tap at regular intervals to check on the pressure gauge. When the required charge is reached, bleed excess air from the system as laid down in the manufacturer's instructions, then carefully remove the probe from the air inlet.

Removable Air Bottle

For the removable air bottle we shall use the BSA Super Ten as our example.

Check the rifle is unloaded and the safety catch is on.

Remove the bottle from the rifle, but do not unscrew too quickly or you will get a sudden release of air and damage the O ring on the bottle. You must first close the valve on the buddy bottle (to do this unscrew the bottle one full turn and no more). To release the air that will now be trapped in the rifle's regulator valve, keep cocking and firing the weapon until the muzzle discharge becomes noticeably quieter. If the discharge does not quieten after dry firing eight to ten times, undo the bottle a further quarter turn and continue firing until it quietens. Once the muzzle discharge has quietened, the regulator has been emptied and it is safe to completely remove the bottle (Step 16). The adaptor is attached to the charging equipment. Then the bottle is screwed into the adaptor. I find that tightening by hand is not sufficient to cause an air seal, so a spanner will be required (Step 17).

Once the bottle is attached to the charging system the procedure is the same as above. The standard 200cc bottle on the Super Ten is charged to 232 bar, but check the bottle to

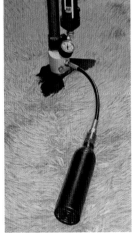

Steps 16 and 17.

make sure that this is the case. The charge pressure will be stamped on the top of the bottle in the following manner, CP232bar.

Once the bottle is correctly charged, remove it from the charging gear as explained above and screw it back into the rifle; but before you do check the O ring around the neck of the bottle. If it is damaged replace it; if not apply a little Molycote 111 grease to it.

SERVICING

About every 12 months a PCP should be sent to a competent gunsmith to be serviced. The service will include having the air reservoir checked internally for corrosion. The importance of this cannot be over-stressed. The air reservoir cannot afford to be subject to serious internal corrosion, as this undermines the reservoir's integrity and renders it possible for the reservoir to rupture, in which case it would explode like a bursting lorry tyre. So have your PCP checked every 12 months without fail. You could have the manufacturer do this or you could send it to a specialist workshop.

THE SCOPE

Fitting a Scope

Remove the top portion of the scope mount rings completely by unscrewing the screws to the left and right of the ring. This is most commonly done with an Allen key. Lay the top portion of the rings and the screws safely to one side.

Fix the base of your mounts to whatever receiving system you have on your rifle – a scope rail or grooves. To do this, check that your rifle is safe, then place it on a bench with the barrel resting on a small sandbag. (I make my own sandbags by filling a plastic bag with some sand until it is about the size of a bag of sugar, then I tape the entire surface of the bag so that the sand cannot escape.)

Loosen the screws in the base of the mounts (they do not have to be completely removed). If one of the mounts has an arrestor pin, it will

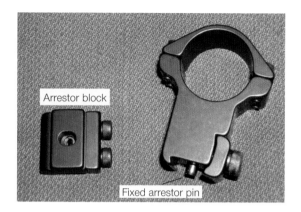

Step 18.

be the rear mount. It goes on the trigger end of the scope rail. If it is a quality Sportsmatch mount, the arrestor pin will be fixed (Step 18) and will need to go into the hole you have had pre-drilled into the scope rail. If it is a screw-down arrestor pin, it will need to be screwed up into the body of the base; then the mount will fit onto the rail. When you attach the base mounts to the scope rail, place them at the position you think is correct and hand tighten them into place (Step 19). Remember that on spring-powered weapons, if you have an arrestor block of some kind the rear mount must be tight up against it.

Lay the scope across the two mounts and see if they are in the correct location: the back mount should be just in front of the

Step 19.

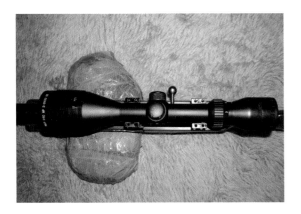

Step 20.

Steps 22 and 23.

magnification ring and the forward mount just in front of the turrets (Step 20). Once the mounts are in the correct place remove the scope and tighten down both mounts. If it is a PCP they need to be just tight; if it is a springer they need to be very tight.

Place a purpose-made spirit level across the mounts to make sure that they are level (such a spirit level can be purchased from Sportsmatch) (Step 21).

If you have a screw-down arrestor pin, screw it down tight on a PCP, very tight on a springer.

Line the rings with a layer of foam (I use foam that is intended as the underlay for wooden flooring) (Steps 22 and 23).

Place the scope across the bottom rings and place the top rings on, remembering to line them also with a layer of foam. The top rings want to be very slightly tightened down.

Raise the rifle to the shoulder and look through the scope. Firstly you want to concern yourself with achieving a clear picture through the scope. If there is a black circle around the outer circumference of the lens, move the scope backwards or forwards by gently rotating it from side to side to move it through the rings. The ocular lens should be about 82–89mm away from your eye, depending on the scope you are using. If it is a Hawke scope, their catalogue will give you the exact eye relief (*see* Step 24 overleaf).

Once you have a clear sight, picture check to see that the horizontal and vertical crosshairs are straight. I point the rifle at the sky and move the scope very slightly to the left or

Step 21.

Step 24.

Step 26.

right, until I am confident the cross-hairs are straight.

All that remains is to tighten down the top rings (Step 25). Screw down the screw on one side a few turns, and do the same to the screw on the opposite side. Repeat the process, alternating between both sides, until they are tightened. On quality rings, as found on Sportsmatch mounts, the top and bottom ring will come together when tightened without causing any damage to the scope tube; these rings are very precisely engineered. But with cheaper rings that do not share this quality, if you overtighten them you will crush the body tube of the scope and could damage its internals.

Cleaning Scope Lenses (Step 26)

Do not go cleaning scope lenses with bits of old cloth: use a specialist cleaning kit. The lenses can be easily scratched if the wrong material is used upon them. Abbey do a very effective lens cleaning kit comprising lens brush, lens cleaning fluid, and lens cloth. The cleaning fluid that Abbey produces not only cleans the lens but helps to protect it. It also improves light transmission. I use this kit to clean my lenses after every hunting expedition.

Take the lens brush and brush away dirt and dust from the objective and ocular lenses. Spray a small quantity of cleaning fluid onto each lens, and wipe away with the lens cloth.

On no account dismantle your scope: if you do you will release the nitrogen inside and ruin it. If your scope needs internal repairs for any reason, arrange to send it back to the manufacturer and let their experts fix it.

USING A CHRONOGRAPH (Step 27)

There are a number of chronographs on the market, but the one I use is the Combro MK4 cb-625. It is simple to use and it is very reliable.

The cb-625 is a sophisticated measuring device, but in order for it to function correctly it must be accurately lined up with the bore.

Step 25.

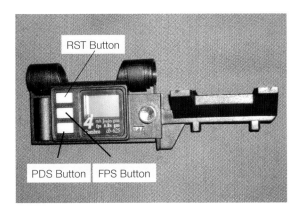

Step 27.

Step 28.

This can be done by eye, but a much more reliable method is to use a bore guide, which goes through the top rings on the cb-625 and into the bore of the rifle to achieve perfect alignment.

In order for the cb-625 to calculate the energy rating of your gun, it first needs to know the weight of the pellet being used in grains (the pellet's weight will be displayed on the tin's lid). To enter this information into the cb-625, press the RST button and hold it down for 14 seconds, at which point a figure will appear with GNS underneath it. This figure is the pellet's weight. When this figure appears, release the RST button. If the weight needs changing press the PDS key to select the figure that needs changing, then use the FPS key to change it.

Make sure that your weapon is unloaded, uncocked, and that the safety is on. Then attach the cb-625 to the end of the barrel. This is done by first loosening the clamp screw so that the V block can slide up or down the barrel freely. Push the bore guide down through the two rings on top of the cb-625, and into the rifle's bore to align the bore with the chronograph; when this is done tighten up the clamp screw.

To hold the cb-625 in place, all that is required is two rubber bands. Slide these over the barrel before you align the cb-625 with the bore. When the cb-625 is aligned simply slide the rubber bands back down the barrel so that they go round the barrel and V block, holding the two together (Step 28).

Remove the bore guide, load the weapon, press the RST key, point the weapon in the air and fire. Apply the safety. Press the PDS button and you will be presented with the gun's energy rating in ft/lb. The display will also read legal if the rating is below 12ft per lb.

Your guns should be tested once a month to ensure that they remain legal. If your gun has gone over the legal limit get the help of a gunsmith to rectify the situation immediately.

One of the good things about the Combro cb-625 is that if anything goes wrong with it then it can be fixed, unlike so many other electronic devices which have to be thrown away when they break.

STRIPPING DOWN THE XL TACTICAL

The purpose of showing you how to strip down the XL Tactical is to demonstrate that a spring-powered gun is a fairly straightforward piece of engineering that can be maintained and repaired by the DIY enthusiast if a little common sense is employed. Although I am using the XL Tactical as my example, the basic procedure is the same for most break barrel weapons (*see* Step 29 overleaf).

First ensure that the gun is unloaded, uncocked and that the safety is on.

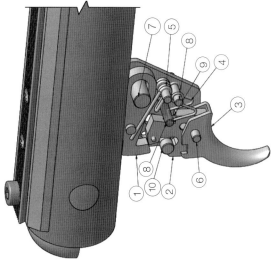
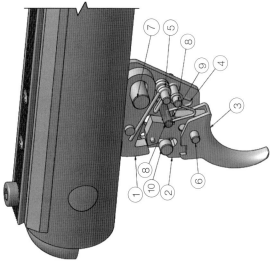

1 Sear
2 Trigger strut
3 Trigger blade
4 Trigger spring
5 Sear spring
6 Trigger axis pin
7 Sear axis pin
8 Pin spring retainer
9 Trigger load adjusting screw
10 Trigger stop pin

1 Lightning cylinder
2 Maxigrip rail
3 Piston seal
4 Piston
5 Piston weight
6 Piston sleeve
7 Mainspring guide
8 End cap location plug
9 Cylinder endcap
10 Mainspring retaining pin
11 Rubber seating strips
12 AT spring guide washer
13 Barrel seal
14 Barrel latch spring

15 Barrel latch pin
16 Slipper plate
17 Slipper plate fixing screw
18 Barrel stop pin
19 Barrel axis pin
20 Cocking link axis pin
21 Scope stop bush
22 Rail stop screw M5×12
23 Main spring
24 22 Lightning XL barrel
25 Cocking link
26 177 Lightning XL barrel
27 25 Lightning XL barrel

Step 29. (Illustrations provided by BSA Guns)

Step 30.

Remove the stock by unscrewing the two screws in the forestock and the one behind the trigger. If they are stiff apply a little WD40 to get them going (Step 30).

Before beginning to disassemble the gun, thoroughly encase the trigger's assembly in tape. I use electrical tape (Step 31). The reason for this is that when you start knocking pins out, the vibration will make the pins in the trigger assembly fall out. As a result the trigger will fall to pieces and, though it is not all that complicated to put back together, it is extremely awkward, especially if you have fat fingers like me; besides, there is no need to dismantle the trigger.

Step 31.

If you take the action you will find a plastic cap at the end of the compression chamber; this simply pulls out (Step 32).

Take an Allen key and undo the screw at the end of the scope rail. Remove the screw

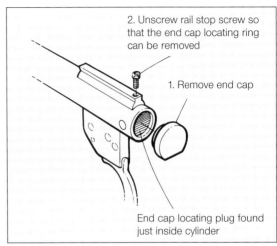

Step 32.

completely and the washer beneath it. If you look down the end of the compression chamber you will see the end-cap-locating plug; if you tip the cylinder up and tap it slightly the plug will fall out.

Remove the barrel by using the correct sized punch and a mallet to knock out the barrel axis pin (the front pin on the breech jaws) (*see* Steps 33 and 34 overleaf).

You are now left with the compression chamber. Now to remove the spring. The spring in the XL Tactical, as it is in all 11.5ft per lb weapons, is very powerful so treat it with respect. Treat the spring in a carefree manner and you may get seriously injured. To remove the spring you will need a spring compressor, which is a tool a bit like a large clamp that has two prongs that stagger the retaining pin; the prongs sit against the mainspring seating washer. The compressor is tightened slightly to take the pressure off the mainspring of the retaining pin, so that it can be removed easily with a punch and mallet. The compressor is now retaining the mainspring. Simply release the mainspring pressure by loosening the compressor until the spring is no longer under compression. I do not have a spring compressor but have converted a sash clamp to do the same job (*see* Steps 35 and 36 overleaf). The spring can now be removed.

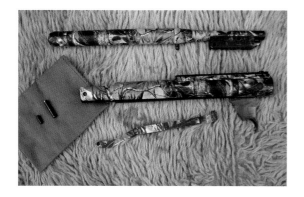

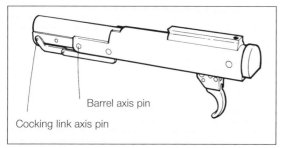

Steps 33 and 34.

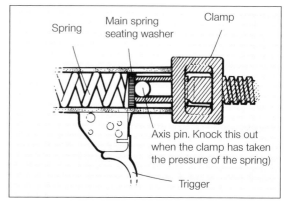

Step 36 (above and top).

Before the piston can be removed, the scope rail has to come off. This is done by placing a piece of wood against the front of the scope rail and giving the wood a number of hefty blows with a mallet.

Turn the compression cylinder upside down and you will see, through the slot in the bottom of the cylinder, the piston. Put a screwdriver through the slot and push the piston back until it stops against the trigger

sear; do not try to force it past the sear, it will not go. Now put your screwdriver in through one of the holes where the scope rail goes and push the sear back and down. Hold it there for a moment; take another screwdriver and put it behind the sear at the back of the trigger mechanism. You should now be able to hold the sear down (Step 37). Remove the screwdriver coming through the hole where the scope goes, and reach into the cylinder with your finger. You will feel the piston; you should be able to slide it out without too much trouble. Once the piston is out, release the sear.

You have now completely dismantled your rifle and can inspect the piston seal, and degrease and relubricate the internals. This will need to be done about every 18 months in order to keep the gun in tiptop condition. If you do not feel up to this yourself, have a gunsmith do it. The other advantage of being able to strip down your gun is that you can repair it yourself

Step 35.

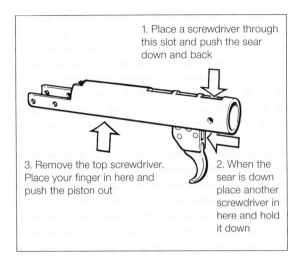

Step 37.

should anything go wrong. To reassemble the weapon, simply reverse the above procedure.

INSTALLING A CUSTOM TUNING KIT (Step 38)

Why should you want to replace the factory mainspring, piston seal and mainspring guide in your gun?

The XL Tactical is the gun version of a Ford Focus: a very reliable, efficient car that can be used day in day out. However, when Ford prepare a Focus for a rally, they take it to a whole new level by substituting factory parts for high-specification components. By doing

Step 38.

this they turn an everyday car into a thorough-bred racing machine. By putting V-Mach custom-made parts inside your spring-powered rifle you do exactly the same thing. V-Mach is a custom rifle workshop that manufactures parts using higher grade materials than are found in factory parts, and machining them to a higher specification.

V-Mach tuning kits are handmade works of engineering art that will turn your spring-powered weapon, whatever it be, into a smooth-operating, more consistent, more friendly weapon with a less violent recoil, greater accuracy and more power – resulting in perfection (and a bigger bag).

Fitting a V-Mach tuning kit is fairly easy for anyone with a reasonable level of mechanical skill. The kit comprises internal components and lubricants.

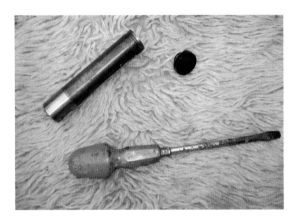

Step 39.

First strip down the rifle as explained above. On the end of the piston there is a piston seal made from plastic; this has to come off. Prise it off with a screwdriver (Step 39).

Clean the inside of the compression cylinder with a clean cloth until every trace of grease is removed, then do the same with the piston inside and out (*see* Steps 40 and 41 overleaf). Follow with the in- and outside cleaning of the piston sleeve.

Put the V-Mach piston seal onto the end of the piston. This is done by centring the seal with the end of the piston, placing a block of

143

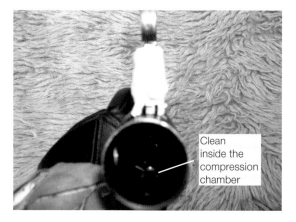

Clean inside the compression chamber

Clean piston inside and out

Steps 40 and 41.

wood over the seal, and tapping it gently into place with a mallet (Step 42).

Turn the piston upside down. You will see a slot. Lightly lubricate it with the grease supplied. The rear of the piston, referred to as the skirt, also needs to be lightly coated with grease. To the circumference of the piston seal you want to apply a barely visible coat of grease, making sure that absolutely none of it gets onto the face of the seal.

Return the piston to the compression cylinder by reversing the procedure used above.

Take one of the washers provided and place it inside the piston. Do not put more than one washer in at this stage or you may well take your gun above the legal limit. Place the piston sleeve inside the piston.

All that remains to be done is to lightly lubricate the mainspring (Step 43), then reassemble the weapon by reversing the procedures above (Step 44). When reassembling the barrel, grease the barrel latch, axis pins and the sides of the breech jaws.

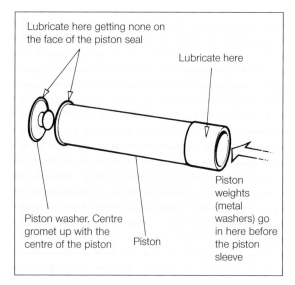

Lubricate here getting none on the face of the piston seal

Lubricate here

Piston washer. Centre gromet up with the centre of the piston

Piston

Piston weights (metal washers) go in here before the piston sleeve

Step 42.

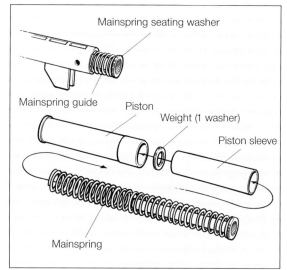

Mainspring seating washer

Mainspring guide

Piston

Weight (1 washer)

Piston sleeve

Mainspring

Step 43.

Step 44.

Step 45.

You now have a top of the range spring-gun that many shooters would give their eye teeth to own.

Before putting the gun back together you could, like me, camouflage it using a special gun tape from a company called Garlands. You simply cut to shape and stick it to the gun (Step 45).

APPENDIX I

The Bazooka

This material is taken from two articles originally published in *Air Gunner* magazine, and provides further insight into my use of the 0.25 calibre BSA XL Tactical.

On the trips I have made out I find that, though I have a cabinet full of guns, my hand is constantly drifting towards one particular weapon: my favourite and the most devastating air gun I have ever handled, which slams its pellet into the quarry like a sledgehammer. The gun I am referring to is a BSA XL Tactical in .25 calibre. Whenever I tell people that my favourite gun is a .25 calibre they look at me is if I have gone mad. The .25 is held in low esteem amongst shooters because they believe all the inaccurate information that has been written and said about this much-maligned and under-utilized calibre. Current thinking leans towards .177 as the ultimate hunting calibre due to its flat trajectory and thus the amazing accuracy that gives the competent shooter the ability to shoot a fly at 30yd, but I am not looking for that kind of accuracy. I want something with sheer brute force and you cannot get more brutal than the .25. My brother refers to my .25 XL Tactical as the 'bazooka' because it is noisy and has the healthiest kick I have ever known in an air rifle, equal to some of the smaller-calibre bullet guns. Some may see this as a disadvantage, but I love the challenge of dealing with such a brute – every single shot is a challenge to the marksmanship that requires consistent technique to be employed from shot to shot.

The .25 is not as accurate as a .177, but if you practise with it you can achieve a 1in grouping. That will not win any prizes on the target side of things, where sub-1in groupings are the norm, but for the hunting field a 1in

The XL Tactical fitted with lasers and a tactical light.

The level of accuracy that can be achieved with .25 calibre.

grouping is more than sufficient for a humane kill. To give you an idea of how accurate the .25 can be, I went shooting recently for just one hour in which time I took thirteen shots and came home with ten feral pigeons and a rabbit. Only two shots missed and one of those was because the pigeon had the good luck to move just as I was squeezing the trigger.

Range is also another area where the .25 has been criticized. Some people would have you believe that you have to be almost on top of your quarry in order to kill it because the heavy 0.25 pellet lacks the velocity to cover any kind of distance, but I have consistently found that the .25 XL Tactical will perform to devastating effect out to distances of 30yd. You have to aim a bit higher than you would with the other calibres, for obvious reasons. So the .25 will take varied quarry at 30yd, which is the maximum distance over which I generally chose to hunt, whatever the calibre. (Though shortly before writing this I successfully took a pigeon at well over 35yd with the .25!)

The thing I most like about the XL Tactical .25 is the sheer force that it is able to unleash. The level of damage this gun can do to the flesh and bone of quarry is far in excess of what the other calibres can achieve. The .22 and .177 are 'surgical', doing very little tissue damage and leaving a wound tract that

resembles a hot knitting needle going into butter; as a result, you need to strike a vital organ such as the brain or heart in order to cause death. The .25 is totally different: it literally pulverises everything it comes into contact with, be that flesh or bone, leaving a devastating wound tract that causes severe haemorrhaging. This means that this calibre can be used to take body shots in pigeons that prove almost instantly fatal.

A .22 or .177 pellet generally leaves an exit wound due to over-penetration that is roughly parallel to the entrance wound, the pellet taking a fairly straight course through the quarry from front to back. When shooting rabbits the .25 does not exit the head due because it dissipates all of its energy on impact, transferring it to the target. As you can see from the photo of a .25 pellet used to kill a rabbit, the pellet not only flattens but folds back on itself, almost like a dum dum bullet, all of the pellet's energy being transferred to the surrounding tissue. This delivers a huge amount of hydraulic shock, like hitting the rabbit in the head with a hammer.

On recovering pellets in .177 and .22 calibre from shot quarry I have found that there is so little distortion in the pellets that they could be loaded back into the gun and fired again. Both these calibres retain much of their energy to travel through the quarry rather than imparting it to the surrounding tissue,

A .25 retrieved from a rabbit. Notice how it is flattened and distorted.

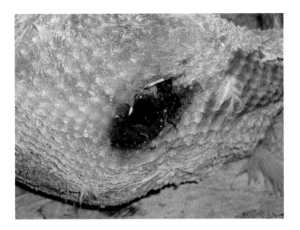

The effect of a .25 pellet on the body of a feral pigeon.

have the luxury of waiting around to get the perfect shot, which is what I would do if I was out hunting. Pest control is all about bringing down as many birds as possible as quickly as possible and with as little disturbance to the farmer and livestock as possible. The pigeon's head is a small target and hitting it in the cluttered, dark environment found on most farms means you have to take your time, the margin for error being minuscule.

The pigeon's body, on the other hand, is a large target that is quite difficult to miss. By 'body' I am referring the area in which the crop, heart, lungs and liver are located, a shot into this region being fatal. Having such

which is why accuracy is such an issue: the pellet really needs to be placed in brain tissue to cause instant, humane death. When I shoot pigeons with a .25 I aim for the heart and lungs (explained overleaf), the entrance wound thus being in the chest area. The exit wound is not as you might expect in the back, parallel to the entrance wound, but it is usually found at the other end of the body, just above the tail feathers. This is because the slower and heavier pellet is easily deflected from its initial trajectory, which sends it bouncing through the pigeon's insides like a pin ball, causing much more damage than the higher velocity .177 or .22. A correctly placed chest shot in a pigeon with a .25 is always fatal: there is no twitching, no flapping of the wings; the pigeon just drops stone dead.

One of the main advantages of the .25 is its phenomenal clout, allowing the shooter to take a body shot if required. You may be wondering why on earth I would want to take a body shot. Nearly all of my shooting is pest-control for various farmers rather than hunting for sport and food. The farmers are not content to see just one or two pigeons removed in an outing: they expect to see a good 10 per cent of the infestation removed each time I visit, which usually means around about twenty birds. With limited time available I have to acquire my targets very rapidly – I do not

The XL Tactical in .25 calibre with a string of pigeons.

The .25 calibre can be used to body-shoot rats.

a large kill zone allows me to acquire my target and take the shot very quickly before moving on to the next pigeon and the next, so that when I enter a barn with twenty or thirty pigeons perched in the rafter I can get four or five of them in the ten seconds or so it takes them to realize what is going on and make their escape. There is no sneaking up on feral pigeons in a large open barn: they have the high ground and eyes that even in the dim gloom see the slightest of movements. You have to step through the doors and start shooting immediately.

Many of the pigeons that I have to shoot are not side-on but front-on, and the only head shot available would be a shot straight between the eyes – not an imposable shot by any means, but far from easy with a rating of about 50/50 for most hunters. When carrying out pest-control operations you need to be taking shots that rate more favourably, around 90/10 meaning that every shot has at least a 90 per cent chance of bringing down the target. With pigeons that are face-on the only way to have such favourable odds is to be able to take a clean body shot and the .25 allows you to do just that. Many of the pigeons

The XL Tactical gets really dirty on its pest control forays.

that I bring down don't even present a head shot: they hide their head in the rafters, working on the principal that if they cannot see me then I cannot do them any harm. All that is on view is the body and if you do not have a calibre that will allow you to select the body as your target you have to leave the shot or hang about waiting for the pigeon to move – both of which are just not feasible options when carrying out typical pest-control work.

My .25 is the BSA XL Tactical, which is easily one of the toughest and most reliable rifles on the market today – though I have found that its accuracy is affected by dirt in the barrel more than some others. The actual dimensions of the rifle are no different externally to the .177 and .22 versions of this rifle, when you begin to use it you soon discover that it is an entirely different beast with a much more gutsy feel. However, the transition from a .177 or .22 to a .25 is not all that easy and it takes a bit of time on the practice range before you begin to get used to the ballistic characteristics of the much bigger pellet.

APPENDIX II

Kill Zones

The diagram below shows the kill zones for the rat and feral pigeon. The photo of the rabbit overleaf can be used as a target. The circles cover the kill zone.

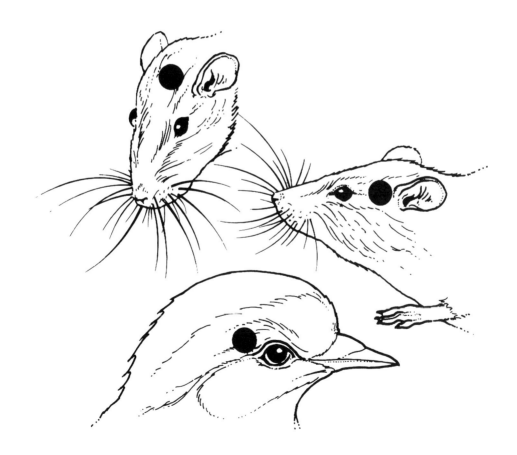

List of Suppliers and Manufacturers

BSA
Manufacturer of high-quality hunting air rifles.
Tel. 0121 722 8543
www.bsaguns.co.uk

Deben Group Industries
Manufacturer and supplier of Hawke scopes and Tracer hunting lamps.
Tel. 0870 4422600
www.deben.com

Whitby & Co.
Supplier of knives.
Tel. 01539 721032
www.whitbyandco.co.uk

Jack Pyke
Manufacturer of camouflage clothing.
Tel. 01234 740327
www.jackpyke.co.uk

Viper and Web-tex
Manufacturer of military equipment.
Tel. 01234 740327
www.viperkit.co.uk
www.web-tex.co.uk

Abbey Supply Company Ltd
Manufacturer of airgun lubricants and cleaning fluids.
Tel. 01202 603067
www.abbeysupply.com

Napier of London
Supplier of cleaning kits and high-quality pellets.
Tel. 01235 812993
www.napier.com

Target Sports of Bolton
Supplier of Predator pellets.
Tel. 0870 060 7331
www.targetsports.co.uk

V-Mach Custom Rifles Ltd
Steve Pope's workshop, where all kinds of air-rifle customizing takes place. If you want anything doing to your rifle this is the place to go.
Tel. 07850 296360

Sportsmatch UK
Manufacturer of the best airgun mounts money can buy.
Tel. 01525 381638
www.sportsmatch-uk.com

Garlands
Supplier of all kinds of gun accessory.
Tel. 01827 383300
www.garlands.uk.com

Glossary

aim point The part of the reticle pattern used to line up the shot.

air reservoir The part of the PCP that holds the air.

anodizing The electrolytic process of coating aluminium to protect it from corrosion.

backstop The part of the range, behind the target, in which the pellets are safely absorbed.

barrel The part of the rifle consisting of a finely machined metal tube down which the pellets travel.

bipod A two-legged stand used to support a rifle.

block The part of the rifle containing the loading mechanism.

bore The inside of the barrel.

breech The end of the barrel that the pellet goes into.

BSA Birmingham Small Arms.

butt The end of the stock that goes into the shoulder.

calibre The diameter of a gun's bore.

carbine A short rifle.

charging gear Equipment used to charge a PCP.

cheekpiece The part of the stock that goes against the cheek.

choke A narrowing of the barrel at the muzzle end.

chronograph A device for measuring velocity.

click A single turn of a scope turret.

cocking The process of getting a rifle ready to discharge by engaging the trigger sear.

cross-hairs Two lines as thin as hairs in a cross shape. These form the reticle pattern.

cylinder The part of the rifle containing the spring piston.

dome head A pellet with a dome head.

eye relief The distance that the eye needs to be from the ocular lens of the scope.

elevation Movement in the horizontal plane.

FAC Fire Arms Certificate.

follow-through The retaining of the shooting position for several seconds after the discharge of the rifle.

forestock The front end of the stock.

FPS Feet per second, a measurement of a projectile's speed.

ft/lb Feet per pound: the measurement of the amount of energy in a projectile.

grouping The placement of shots in a cluster.

gunsmithing The maintenance and repair of weapons.

hollow point A pellet with a concave head.

kill zone The area of an animal's body into which the pellet must be placed to achieve a humane kill.

legal limit The limit to the degree of power that a weapon may possess before an FAC is required. (The current limit is 12ft/lb.)

magazine A storage facility containing pellets so that they can be fed into the barrel.

mainspring The compression spring of a spring-powered gun.

MAP Multi-aim point. A pattern of reticle with numerous aim points for different distances.

mil dot A form of reticle that has dots on the windage and elevation cross-hairs, the dots being used as aim points and as a measuring device to calculate range.

MOA Minutes of angle. A form of measurement used for zeroing scopes giving 1in (2.5cm) of movement at 100yd (91m).

mounts Attachments to clamp a scope onto a gun.

muzzle blast The noise made as the projectile exits the muzzle.

objective lens The lens at the far (barrel) end of the scope.
ocular lens The lens that you look through (at the stock end of the scope).

parallax setting The range at which the scope is set up to function.

PCP Pre-charged pneumatic.

pellet Airgun ammunition.

pointed head A pellet with a pointed head.

range The distance from the shooter to the target.

recoil The rearward movement of a rifle in response to its being discharged.

respiratory pause A momentary ceasing of the breathing just prior to and during the taking of a shot.

reticle The pattern used to make up the scope's aiming grid (for example cross-hairs).

safety catch A catch that locks the trigger.

scope rail A receiving rail for scope mounts.

sear A catch that holds back the trigger.

silencer A device for reducing muzzle blast.

springer A spring-powered weapon.

stock The part of a gun that enables you to hold and shoulder the weapon.

stock weld The point at which the stock and and the shooter's cheek come together.

trajectory The flight path of a projectile.

turret The adjusting mechanism for a scope.

velocity The speed of a projectile.

wad cutter A flat-headed pellet.

windage Lateral adjustment of scopes dictated by wind speed.

wobble Involuntary body movement that is transmitted to the rifle.

zero The point at which a scope is calibrated to your eye.

Index